Challenge Word Games
Through the Year

Grades 6-8

by
Norm Sneller

Published by Instructional Fair
an imprint of
Frank Schaffer Publications®

if

Instructional Fair

Author: Norm Sneller
Editors: Linda Kimble, Lisa Hancock, Sharon Kirkwood
Interior Artist: Randy Rider

Frank Schaffer Publications®

Instructional Fair is an imprint of Frank Schaffer Publications.

Printed in the United States of America. All rights reserved. Limited Reproduction Permission: Permission to duplicate these materials is limited to the person for whom they are purchased. Reproduction for an entire school or school district is unlawful and strictly prohibited. Frank Schaffer Publications is an imprint of School Specialty Publishing. Copyright © 1998 School Specialty Publishing.

Send all inquiries to:
Frank Schaffer Publications
8720 Orion Place
Columbus, Ohio 43240-2111

Challenge Your Mind: Word Games Throughout the Year—grades 6-8

ISBN: 1-56822-665-9

8 9 10 11 PAT 12 11 10 09

Table of Contents

New Year's Day (January 1)
   Party Time (spelling) 4
   Bring on the New! (spelling) 5
Twelfth Day (January 5)
   It's the 12th Day! (spelling) 6
Charles Perrault's Birthday (January 12)
   Name the Author (inference) 7
A.A. Milne's Birthday (January 18)
   Hello, Pooh! (spelling) 8
Robert E. Lee Day (January 19)
   The Gentleman General (research) 9
Martin Luther King Jr., Day (third Monday in January)
   I Have a Dream Today (spelling) 10
First Basketball Game (December, 1891)
   We Are the Champions! (problem-solving matrix) 11
Black History Month (February)
   Wade in the Water, Children (vocabulary) 12
Groundhog Day (February 2)
   Wake Up! (vocabulary) 13
Mardi Gras (Shrove Tuesday—day before Lent)
   A Wild Carnival (vocabulary) 14
Inventors Day (February 11)
   Brand Spankin' New (vocabulary) 15
Lincoln's Birthday (February 12)
   Honest Abe (vocabulary) 16
Presidents' Day (third Monday in February)
   Hail to the Chief (vocabulary) 17
Marian Anderson's Birthday (February 17)
   The Beautiful Voice (vocabulary) 18
Washington's Birthday (February 22)
   Hey, No Lie! (vocabulary) 19
Ramadan (ninth month of the Islamic year–date varies)
   Revealed by Gabriel (context clues) 20
Spring
   Celebrating the New Life (vocabulary) .. 21
Purim (February or March)
   When a Girl Saved Her People (spelling) 22
The Doll's Festival (March 3)
   Rock-A-Bye (spelling) 23
St. Patrick's Day (March 17)
   Go Gaelic! (sentence structure) 24
   Th' Luck o' the Irish (inference) 25
   The Wearin' o' the Green (spelling) 26
First Day of Spring (vernal equinox)
   Rite of Spring or Stravinsky's Revenge (vocabulary) 27
Easter/Passover (March or April)
   Spring Madness (problem-solving matrix) 28
   Easter Words (synonyms) 29
   Homophonic Homily (homophones) 30
April Fools' Day (April 1)
   Whiz-Dumb? (spelling) 31
Arbor Day (date varies by state)
   Treed Me Right! (vocabulary) 32
Be Kind to Animals Week (first full week of May)
   A Toast to Critters (vocabulary) 33
Tax Day (April 15)
   Giving to Caesar (vocabulary) 34
Patriot Day (April 16)
   On to Lexington! (vocabulary) 35
Shakespeare's Birthday (April 23)
   All Is Mended (literature) 36
   Bow to the Bard (spelling) 37
Bird Day (March 21)
   Singing Sweetly, (Sometimes) (vocabulary) 38
May Day (May 1)
   Hail, Bounteous May! (synonyms) 39
Wesak (May 9)
   Birthday for Buddha (spelling) 40
Mother's Day (second Sunday in May)
   Mom and Me (spelling) 41
   Words Cannot Describe (but I'll try) (vocabulary) 42
Florence Nightingale's Birthday (May 12)
   The Lady with the Lamp (vocabulary) ... 43
Memorial Day (May 30, or the last Monday in May)
   We Salute You! (spelling) 44
   We Remember (vocabulary) 45
Pan American Day (April 14)
   The Picture-esque Americas (inference) 46
Flag Day (June 14)
   Wave Your Flag High (spelling) 47
Father's Day (third Sunday in June)
   G'mornin', Poppa! (synonyms) 48
First Day of Summer (summer solstice)
   Warm and Sunny (vocabulary) 49
   A Simmerin' Summer (problem-solving matrix) 50
Helen Keller's Birthday (June 27)
   Overcoming Adversity (context clues) ... 51
Summer Vacation
   In Praise of Summer (spelling) 52
Canada Day (July 1)
   The Great North Country (vocabulary) . 53
U.S. Independence Day (July 4)
   You're a Grand Old Flag! (vocabulary) .. 54
   At the Bridge (context clues) 55
Bastille Day (July 14)
   On This Day (context clues) 56
National Ice-Cream Day (third Sunday in July)
   We All Scream for Ice Cream (spelling) . 57
First Landing on Moon (July 20)
   Lunar Madness (vocabulary) 58
Pied Piper Anniversary (July 22)
   Beware the Flute Player! (synonyms) ... 59
Raksha Bandhan (July or August)
   Brother and Sister (problem-solving matrix) 60
Hiroshima Day (August 6)
   The Flash (vocabulary) 61
Klondike Gold Discovery Day (August 17)
   Panning in the Wild (context clues) 62
America's Cup (date varies)
   Well, Blow Me Down! (spelling) 63
19th Amendment Day (August 18)
   Being Equal (context clues) 64
First Day of School
   Farewell, Summer! (spelling) 65
Labor Day (first Monday in September)
   Career Caper (spelling) 66
National Grandparents Day (first Sunday in September following Labor Day)
   Your Not-So-Distant Past (vocabulary) ... 67
Mickey Mouse's Birthday (November 18)
   See You Real Soon (vocabulary) 68

Post Office Anniversary of Opening (November 5)
   Mr. Postman, Look and See (vocabulary) 69
First Day of Autumn (autumnal equinox)
   It's a (Cold) Snap! (vocabulary) 70
International Day of Peace (third Tuesday of September)
   Grant Us Peace (vocabulary) 71
Johnny Appleseed's Birthday (September 26)
   Grapple with Apples (spelling) 72
Sukkoth (September or October)
   A Season to Praise (vocabulary) 73
Fire Prevention Week (early October)
   A Hot Time in the Old Town Tonight (antonyms) 74
Columbus Day (second Monday in October)
   Charting the Explorers (vocabulary) 75
   Explor-a-tion (vocabulary) 76
Noah Webster's Birthday (October 16)
   Papa Wordsmith (spelling) 77
United Nations Day (October 24)
   We Are the World (vocabulary) 78
   Know Your World (vocabulary) 79
Halloween (October 31)
   Things That Go Bump (spelling) 80
   A Frightful Custom (context clues) 81
Diwali (October or November)
   Hindu Festival of Lights (spelling) 82
All Saints' Day (November 1, or the first Sunday of Pentecost)
   Add or Subtract (vocabulary) 83
Author's Day (November 1)
   Writer's Niche (vocabulary) 84
National Sandwich Day (November 3)
   I'll Have a Dagwood, Please (synonyms) 85
Election Day (first Tuesday after the first Monday of November)
   Bring on the New! (problem-solving matrix) 86
   Crazy Cryptics (vocabulary) 87
Veterans Day (November 11)
   Over There! (synonyms) 88
Thanksgiving (last Thursday in November)
   A Picture's Worth ... (picture clues) 89
   A Thanksgiving Puzzle (vocabulary) 90
   Turkey Time (vocabulary) 91
Hanukkah (December)
   Festival of Lights (vocabulary) 92
St. Nicholas Day (December 6)
   A Right Jolly Fellow (spelling) 93
Wright Brothers First Flight (December 17)
   Fly Away Home (vocabulary) 94
First Day of Winter (winter solstice)
   Northern Climes (vocabulary) 95
Christmas (December 25)
   Ho, Ho ... Oh No! (vocabulary) 96
   Sing Lullaby (synonyms) 97
   Sing We Merrily (vocabulary) 98
   What Child Is This? (spelling) 99
   Christmas Superstitions in Threes (context clues) 100
Kwanzaa (December 26–January 1)
   Community Building (context clues) 101
   An African Tradition Returns (spelling) . 102
New Year's Eve (December 31)
   10 ... 9 ... 8 ... (vocabulary) 103
Answer Key 104–128

Party Time

name _____

New Year's Day

Unscramble these words and phrases to identify well known New Year's Day items.

1. big march of people and floats in California

    t t m n n a u e o r   f o   s o r s e   e r p d a a

    _____

2. a two-faced god from Roman mythology for whom we name this month

    s a u n j _____

3. a macho viewing which dominates this afternoon

    t l a o b l o f   s g e a m _____

4. something often made in this merry season but seldom kept

    t s s o o i u l r e n _____

5. this is how the holiday begins in New York City

    l a b l   p d o r _____

6. obnoxious non-musical instruments of noise

    r y t a p   a s r v f o _____

7. a sparkling display of sound and sight

    k r r e o s i f w _____

8. a musical offering which memorializes the good old days

    d u a l   n g a l   y e n s _____

9. beverage made of products from chicken, cow, and cane

    o g e g n g _____

10. the Chinese New Year's Day, often later in year, celebrates this for each person

    y t i a d r h b _____

© Instructional Fair • TS Denison

IF8728 *Challenge Your Mind*

Bring on the New!

Name _____

New Year's Day

Fit the letters in each column into the boxes directly above them to form words. The letters may or may not go into the boxes in the same order in which they are given. Your finished puzzle is a translation from a Japanese poem about the new year.

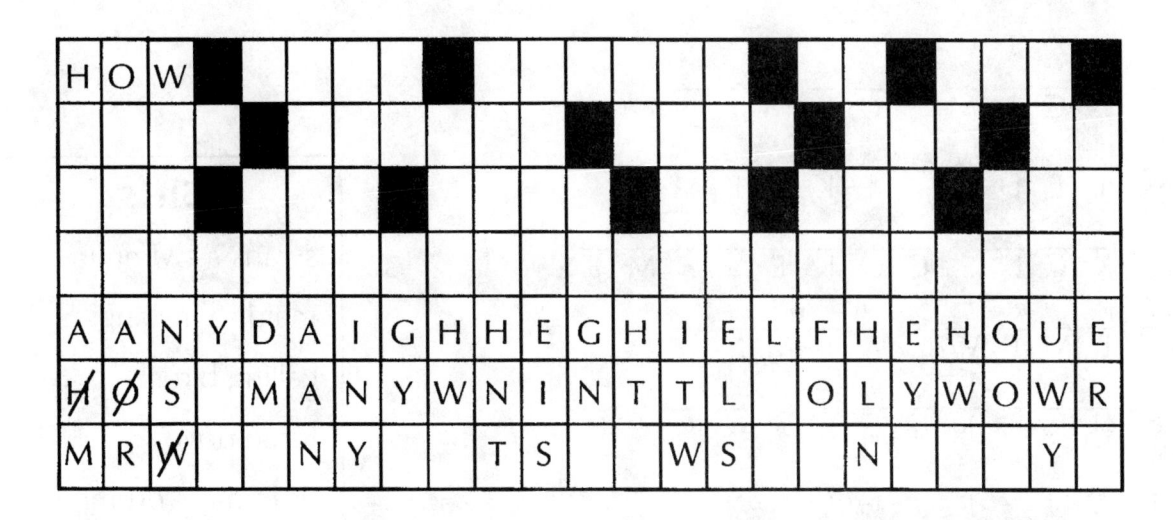

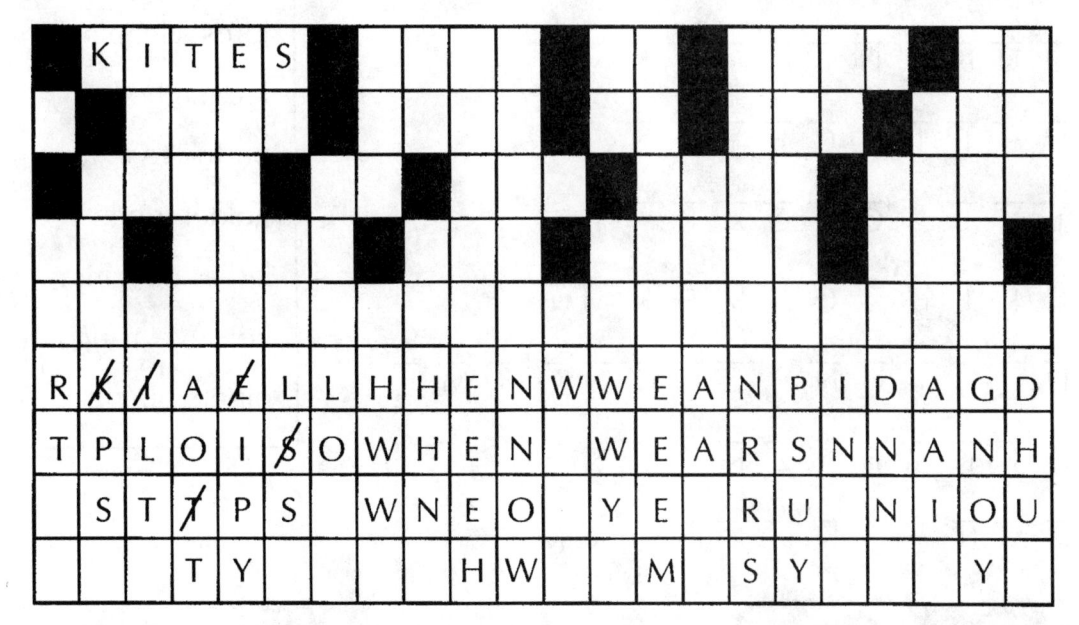

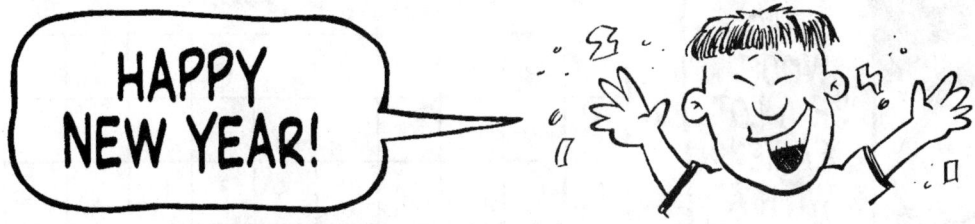

HELPFUL HINTS: It may be helpful to determine the smallest words first and cross the letters off as you use them. Also, two words will wrap to a second line.

HAPPY NEW YEAR!

© Instructional Fair • TS Denison

IF8728 *Challenge Your Mind*

It's the 12th Day!

name _____

January 6 is known as "the twelfth day of Christmas." In many places around the world, gifts are exchanged on this day to honor the memory of the gifts of the Wise Men, long ago. Here are the twelve gifts from the song *The Twelve Days of Christmas*. Can you determine the code and decipher the names of the presents?

a. F B E C L M   U K M F N

b. T K T L U N   T K T K M F

c. Q G K C N   G Q K E V K M F

d. S U L M P W   W L M N

e. T G U R U K C F L   K M   G   T L G U   R U L L

f. E B U C N   G E L G T K M F

g. R D U R E L   C B Y L N

h. F L L N L   G E G A K M F

i. E G C K L N   C G M P K M F

j. C U D Q Q L U N   C U D Q Q K M F

k. P G E E K M F   Z K U C N

l. N H G M N   G N H K Q Q K M F

Gifts
swans a-swimming
maids a-milking
calling birds
turtle doves
drummers drumming
lords a-leaping
French hens
partridge in a pear tree
golden rings
ladies dancing
geese a-laying
pipers piping

THIS WOULD BE A LOT EASIER WITH A DECODER RING!

CODE

A	B	C	D	E	F	G	H	I	J	K	L	M

N	O	P	Q	R	S	T	U	V	W	X	Y	Z

© Instructional Fair • TS Denison

IF8728 *Challenge Your Mind*

Name the Author

name _____

Mystery Author

This 17th century writer is best known for the fairy tales he wrote. He also compiled a book of *Mother Goose* rhymes before the English did. To find his name, figure out the titles or first lines of each rhyme. He authored versions of the four stories, but the eleven rhymes are ancient lore with uncertain origins.

1. an accident-prone H_2O-obtaining pair on a tumble
2. an oval unborn chick topples and breaks his shell
3. a wool producer of dark hue who bleats
4. a maiden with minuscule feet who reposes by the fire
5. a happy monarch requests his comforts—including some tobacco
6. a frustrated mother who lives in a leather home begets too many offspring
7. a wise, galoshes-wearing feline
8. this barnyard thief is the son of a flautist
9. a feline violinist is joined by a menagerie and tableware
10. a Halloween gourd chomper
11. a trusting child strolls off to visit her sick grandmother
12. The beautiful maiden who pricked her finger and was kissed
13. three merchants floating in an open barrel
14. a dairy product's sipper is appalled by a friendly arachnid
15. five petite porkers

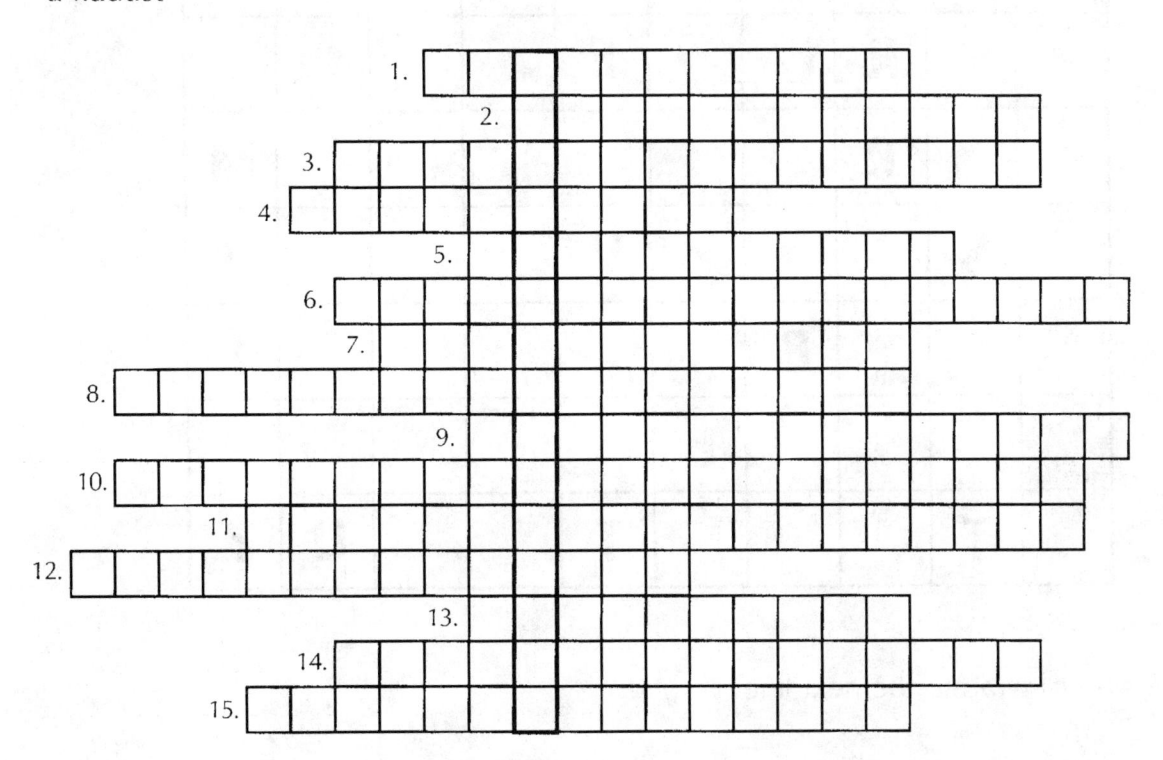

© Instructional Fair • TS Denison

IF8728 *Challenge Your Mind*

Hello, Pooh!

name _____

A.A. Milne's Birthday

Fill in the diagram with the words listed to form a quotation from A. A. Milne's *Winnie the Pooh*. The quotation will read from left to right. Included are letters to assist you.

What does Pooh say while knocking on Rabbit's door?

A.A. MILNE ALSO WROTE "THE RED HOUSE MYSTERY" IN 1921!

Word List

be	isn't	rabbit	that
because	must	said	there
hallo	must	somebody	there
have	nobody	somebody	you

	H								B
			M						Y
		R				E			
		O							M
	S				V				I
			B						L
					B				
			T			T		U	?

Hint: Some words will wrap to the next line.

© Instructional Fair • TS Denison

IF8728 *Challenge Your Mind*

The Gentleman General

name _____

Robert E. Lee Day

Discover facts about the remarkable soldier Robert E. Lee. The letters in the bold boxes of the completed puzzle will tell you even more. Use an encyclopedia or other information source if you're stumped.

1. In July of 1863, his army was forced to leave this Pennsylvania town.
2. At this battle, Lee had his greatest success and greatest loss.
3. This is the war for which Lee is most well-known.
4. The name of the South's president was Jefferson _____.
5. Lee's wife was the great-granddaughter of _____ (Custis) Washington.
6. This was Lee's army rank.
7. The Southern states formed this union.
8. After the war Lee became president of _____ College (it now includes his name).
9. Here Lee commanded the Federal troops as they subdued John Brown's raid.
10. Lee's dad, Henry, was a cavalry officer nicknamed "Light _____ _____."
11. He served as officer in this war alongside General Scott.
12. This is the state Lee served faithfully.
13. Lee's great friend who died serving him, was _____ Jackson.
14. Lee's father fought in this war.
15. Lee received his training at this school.

ROBERT E. LEE WAS BORN ON JANUARY 19, 1807!

HIS FATHER WAS "LIGHT HORSE HARRY" LEE!

© Instructional Fair • TS Denison

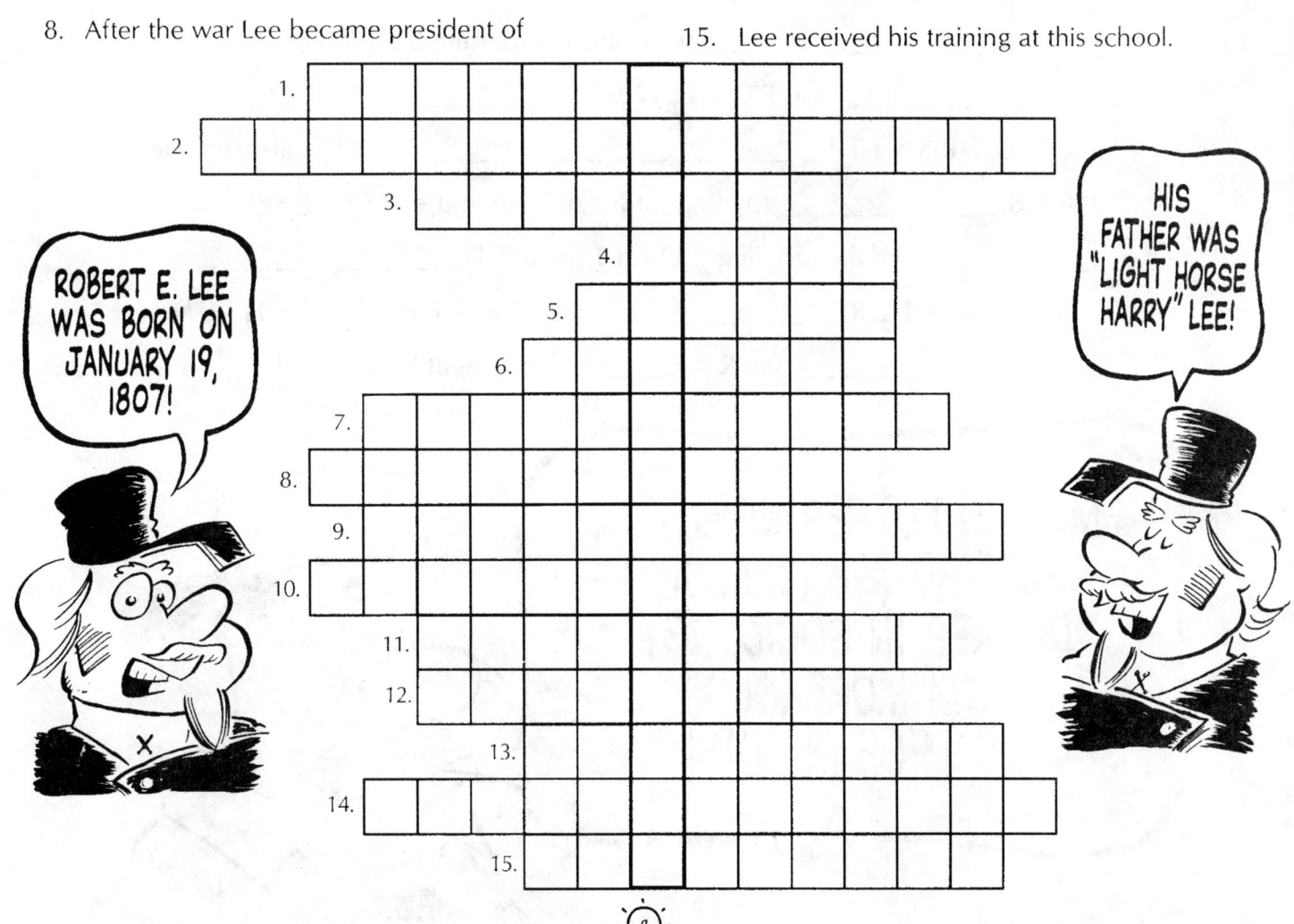

IF8728 Challenge Your Mind

I Have a Dream Today

name _____

Martin Luther King, Jr., Day

Unscramble the bold-faced letters below to complete words from this segment of Martin Luther King, Jr.'s, famous speech.

When we let **D E E F M O R** _____ ring, when we let it **G I N R** _____ from every **A E G I L L V** _____ and every hamlet, from every state and every **Y I T C** _____ , we will be able to **D E P E S** _____ up that day when all of God's **C D E H I L N R** _____ , **A B C K L** _____ men and white men, **S E J W** _____ and **E E G I L N S T** _____ , **A E N O P R S S T T T** _____ and Catholics, will be **L A E B** _____ to join hands and sing in the **D O R S W** _____ of the old Negro **U A I I L P R S T** _____ , "Free at last! **E F E R** _____ at last! Thank God **T A G Y H I L M** _____ , we **R A E** _____ free at last!"

> MARTIN LUTHER KING, JR., RECEIVED A BACHELOR'S DEGREE IN SOCIOLOGY FROM MOREHOUSE COLLEGE IN 1948!

© Instructional Fair • TS Denison

IF8728 *Challenge Your Mind*

We Are the Champions!

name _____

First Basketball game

Early and his teammates won the all-school co-ed basketball tournament in Hoosierville, Indinoisigan. (Ever hear of it?) Early's male teammates are Arvell and Derek. The straight-shooting girl teammates are Fiona, Bonnie, and Carly. No two players scored the same number of points nor committed the same number of fouls although one player did foul out. Use the clues below to match each player with the points scored and the fouls committed.

Hint: Once you record a yes (y) in a box, write no (n) in all the boxes in that row and column.

Clues:

1. The girl who scored nine points had no fouls. Derek had four points and an even number of fouls.

2. Fiona scored more points than Bonnie who scored one more point than a boy. This boy outscored another teammmate.

3. Two girls closed with the highest scores. They had either 2 or 5 fouls.

4. The 11-point male closed with 3 fouls. Carly scored the most points.

5. Fiona had one less foul than Early.

I DON'T THINK THE BULLS HAVE ANYTHING TO WORRY ABOUT!

	Points Scored						Fouls Committed					
Team	4	8	9	11	12	14	0	1	2	3	4	5
Arvell												
Bonnie												
Carly												
Derek												
Early												
Fiona												

© Instructional Fair • TS Denison

IF8728 *Challenge Your Mind*

Wade in the Water, Children

name _____

Black History Month

Here are the names of 20 important black Americans. Match each one with his or her description.

Name List

Bill Cosby
Rosa Parks
W.E.B. DuBois
Martin Luther King
Malcolm X
Mohammed Ali
Jesse Jackson
L. Douglas Wilder
Thurgood Marshall
Shirley Chisholm
Tom Bradley
Leontyne Price
Guion S. Bluford
Langston Hughes
Spike Lee
Jackie Robinson
Booker T. Washington

1. first black in professional baseball
2. a founder of the N.A.A.C.P
3. first black Supreme Court justice
4. early female black representative in U.S. House
5. first black mayor of Los Angeles
6. ran in presidential primary in '84
7. comedian and television sit-com star
8. first black astronaut in space
9. early black educator; preached patience
10. Baptist minister; preached non-violence
11. black Muslim leader who called for a social revolution
12. refused to give up her bus seat
13. filmmaker
14. a Harlem Renaissance poet
15. female opera singer
16. first black governor
17. sting-like-a-butterfly boxer

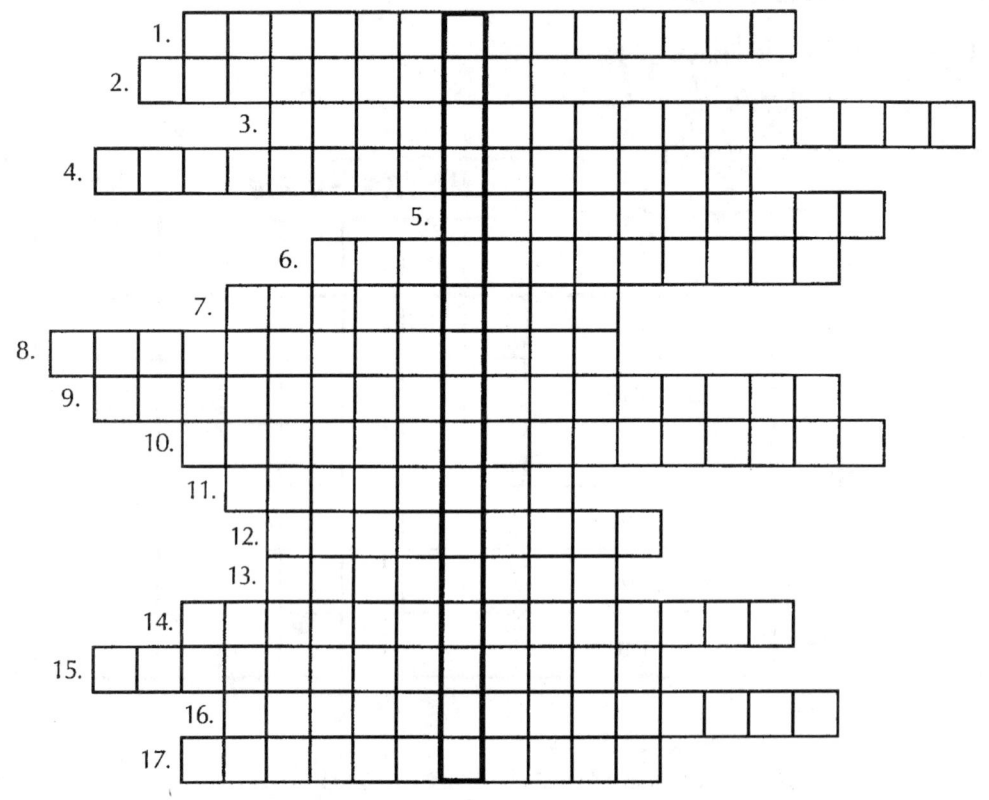

© Instructional Fair • TS Denison

IF8728 *Challenge Your Mind*

Wake Up!

Name _____

Groundhog Day

Insert the 22 letters from the letter bank into the empty boxes to form words relating to the groundhog. The letter you insert may be the first, the last, or in the middle of the word. Cross out letters in the letter bank as you use them. **Note:** Not all letters in each row are used to form words! The completed puzzle will state a fact about this furry creature.

T	S	W	I	N		E	R	F	T
G	F	L	E	C		E	W	A	S
M	A	W	A	K		N	D	L	E
W	A	S	N	O		Z	Z	E	D
B	M	A	R	M		T	M	U	D
U	S	E	L	F		L	K	A	M
S	F	I	E	L		N	C	E	D
E	C	O	P	L		U	R	L	B
S	W	E	I	G		T	T	E	N
C	R	O	E	S		N	G	C	E
E	T	O	P	A		R	O	W	D
R	G	R	O	C		T	A	L	K
D	U	N	C	S		A	D	O	W
C	H	A	T	H		C	K	M	X
T	H	U	M	B		R	O	W	N
Y	T	H	E	M		R	G	E	F
W	E	B	U	R		O	W	O	W
U	G	R	O	U		D	O	I	S
F	L	O	W	E		T	H	E	R
R	O	D	E	N		E	L	Y	M
V	A	N	S	L		E	P	S	U
S	C	L	U	M		Y	Q	U	E

Speech bubble: "KEEP IT DOWN, WILL YA?! I'M TRYING TO GET SOME SLEEP HERE!!"

Letter Bank

A	B	C	C	D	E	E	E
H	H	H	I	K	N	O	O
R	S	T	T	U	W		

© Instructional Fair • TS Denison

IF8728 *Challenge Your Mind*

A Wild Carnival

name _____

Mardi Gras

Mardi Gras is a festive holiday with a very old history. Its celebration combines aspects of Christian, ancient Egyptian, and Roman traditions.

Match each word from the Word Box to its definition. The letter boxes may help you do this more easily.

Word Box

band	dancers	fat Tuesday	masquerade	Rex	parades
carne vale	Epiphany	float	New Orleans	Shrovetide	
costume	Fast Nacht	pageantry	Pancake Day		

1. "farewell meat"
2. the U.S. center for this holiday festival
3. to pretend or to disguise oneself
4. the fanciful clothing of a Mardi Gras reveller
5. the French translation of "Mardi Gras"
6. those whose body movements follow a pattern of rhythm and music
7. the German name for this day; also the name for its rectangular doughnuts
8. a company of musicians
9. the 3 days of confession for past sins
10. the English name for this day; a time to dispense with eggs, milk, and fat
11. a low, flat-topped car/wagon used in parades
12. holy day that begins this season
13. king of the New Orleans carnival
14. a splendid display of pomp
15. huge, colorful processions in this festival

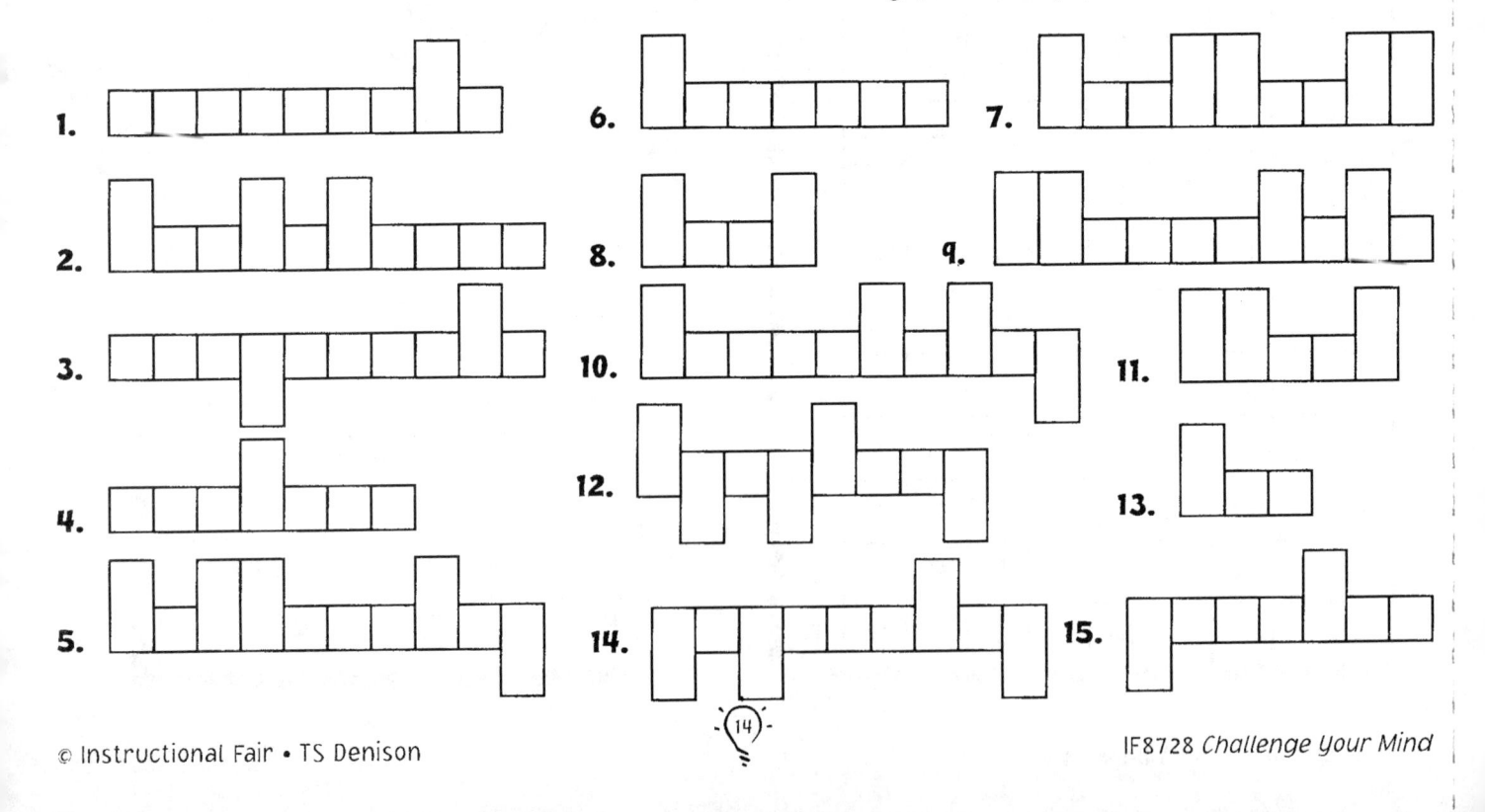

© Instructional Fair • TS Denison

IF8728 *Challenge Your Mind*

Brand Spankin' New

name _____

Inventors Day

February 11 has been named Inventors Day in honor of Thomas Edison's birthday. For each inventor you'll find letters encircling the name. Use these letters to discover what the person invented.

Robert Fulton	Jacques Cousteau	Ladislao Biro
Sergei Korolev	Johan Vaaler	Nikolaus Otto
John Harington	Garrett Morgan	Chester Carlson
Thomas Edison	Evangelista Torricelli	Dennis Gabor
Chester Greenwood	Samuel Morse	J.B.L. Foucault

© Instructional Fair • TS Denison

IF8728 Challenge Your Mind

Honest Abe

Name _____

Lincoln's Birthday

After completing each word pair or compound word, fill in the puzzle. The first one is done for you. Read the highlighted box vertically to learn something about this famous American.

1. _Honest_ Abe
2. Springfield, _____
3. sweet _____
4. top _____
5. bean _____
6. copper _____
7. _____ and south
8. John Wilkes _____
9. _____ Ferry
10. public _____
11. Civil _____
12. Fort _____
13. White _____
14. log _____
15. dire _____
16. Gettysburg _____
16. congress _____
18. Ford _____

Speech bubble: ABRAHAM LINCOLN BECAME A LAWYER IN 1836...

Speech bubble: ...AND WAS MARRIED TO MARY TODD ON NOVEMBER FOURTH, 1842!

1. H O N E S T

© Instructional Fair • TS Denison

IF8728 Challenge Your Mind

Hail to the Chief

name _____

Presidents' Day

Find out about two U.S. presidents. To solve the puzzles, write the name of each picture. Use the numbers below the spaces to help you solve each president's "formula."

__ __ __ __   __ __ __ __ __ __   __ __ __ __
18 11 15 6   1 22 12 5 21 8   4 16 13 9

THEODORE ROOSEVELT WAS THE FIRST PRESIDENT OF THE TWENTIETH CENTURY... ...WHO IS THE LAST?

Franklin D. Roosevelt

__ __ __ __   __ __ __
19 2 17 10   3 14 7 20

__ __ __ __ __   __ __ __ __ __ __
11 22 18 12 8   20 11 14 3 15 9 8 10

__ __ __ __ __ __ __ __ __   __ __ __ __ __ __ __ __ __
6 9 2 8 15 4 22 17 10 13 17   19 7 1 14 5 15 8 15 16 17

__ __ __ __   __ __ __ __   __ __ __ __ __ __   __ __ __ __ __ __
13 29 6 16   11 24 12 7   17 23 1 28 21 2   9 27 18 4 19 8

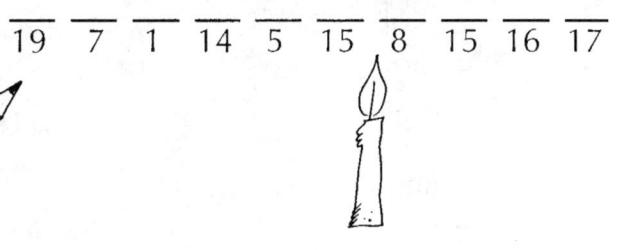

James Garfield

__ __ __   __ __ __
14 10 22   20 5 26

__ __ __   __ __ __ __ __   __ __ __ __ __ __ __ __   __ __ __ __ __ __
24 14 29   2 27 11 20   17 16 8 11 21 4 29 18 20   13 26 7 18

__ __ __   __ __ __ __   __ __ __ __ __
21 1 6   19 10 22   9 12 13 21 18

The Beautiful Voice

name _____

Marian Anderson's Birthday

Fill in the blanks using choices from the Word Bank to learn more about this great singer.

Word Bank

arranged	hall	people	Toscanini
at	inauguration	perform	voice
before	Memorial	permitted	when
black	Metropolitan	remarked	years
Eisenhower	once	steps	York

Marian Anderson was the first _____ singer to _____ at the _____ Opera House in New _____ City. She sang for Arturo _____ . He _____ that she had "a _____ that comes only _____ in a hundred _____ ." In 1939, _____ Anderson was not _____ to sing _____ one music _____ , Eleanor Roosevelt _____ for her to sing _____ 75,000 _____ outdoors on the _____ of the Lincoln _____ . She sang at the _____ balls of both Presidents _____ and Kennedy. She died in 1993 at the age of 91.

Write eight words to describe singing voices using the letters of Ms. Anderson's surname.

A _____
N _____
D _____
E _____
R _____
S _____
O _____
N _____

MARIAN ANDERSON RECEIVED A KENNEDY CENTER HONOR IN 1978!

© Instructional Fair • TS Denison

IF8728 Challenge Your Mind

Hey, No Lie!

Name _____

Combine letter groups to complete words that fit the phrases below. The first one is done for you. It will help to cross off letter groups as you use them.

1. Washington's nickname — *Father of His Country*
2. colony in which Washington was born _____
3. the peace-time profession for which George received training _____
4. Washington's plantation estate _____
5. the wife of Washington _____
6. America's struggle against Great Britain _____
7. what Americans hoped to receive from Great Britain _____
8. in 1876, Congress granted Washington this highest military title _____
9. the political organization which elected him as its presiding officer was the Constitutional _____
10. Washington took this office in 1789 _____

Letter Groups

a	~~fa~~	~~of~~	tion
al	gen	or	tion
con	gi	pen	tis
~~coun~~	~~his~~	pre	~~try~~
cus	lu	re	ven
cy	mar	si	ver
de	mou	sur	vey
den	ni	tha	vir
dence	non	~~ther~~	vo
er	nt	in	

GEORGE WASHINGTON WAS APPOINTED SURVEYOR OF CULPEPPER COUNTY IN 1749 AND THAT'S THE TRUTH!

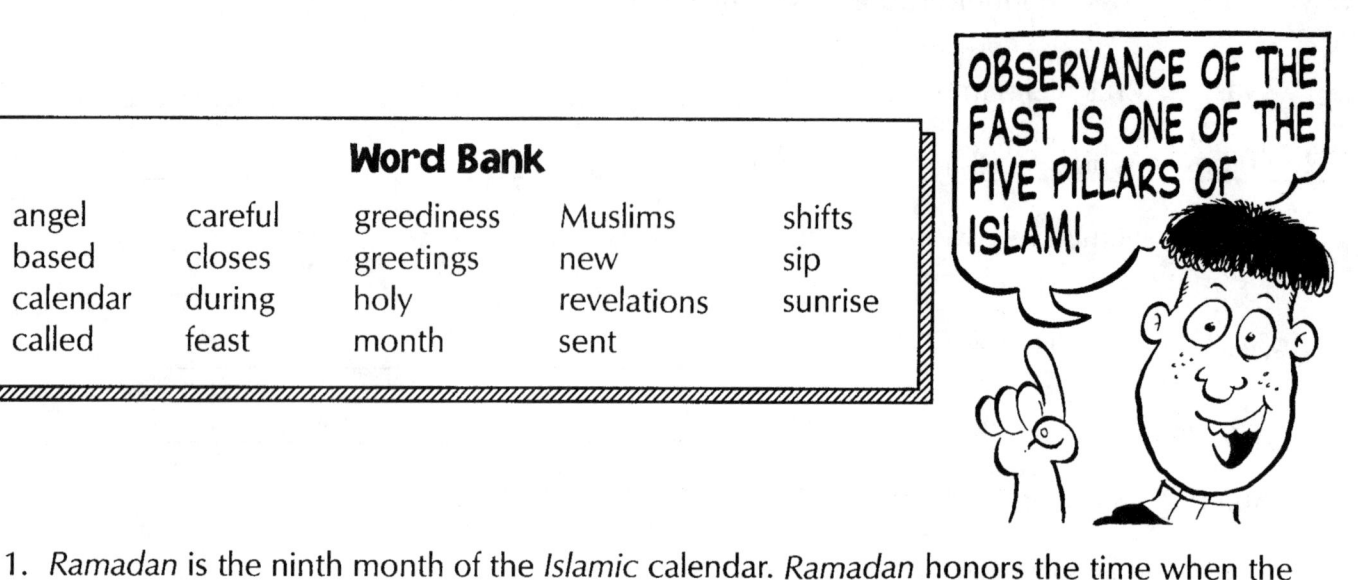

Revealed by Gabriel

name _____

Ramadan

Use context clues to fill in the blanks below with words from the Word Bank.

Word Bank

angel	careful	greediness	Muslims	shifts
based	closes	greetings	new	sip
calendar	during	holy	revelations	sunrise
called	feast	month	sent	

OBSERVANCE OF THE FAST IS ONE OF THE FIVE PILLARS OF ISLAM!

1. *Ramadan* is the ninth month of the *Islamic* calendar. *Ramadan* honors the time when the _____ *Gabriel* made _____ to *Muhammad*.

2. _____ believe that God _____ down the *Koran* during this month.

3. The *Koran* is the most _____ book of the *Islamic* faith.

4. *Muslims* fast from _____ to sunset during this entire month.

5. They may not even have a _____ of water _____ this daytime fast.

6. During *Ramadan* one must be most _____ . Lying, slandering, and _____ may undo the penance of the fast.

7. A three-day festival _____ 'Id al-Fitr _____ this month.

8. During this _____ families gather to pray and give gifts to one another.

9. *Muslims* celebrate the closing feast with _____ clothes and warm _____ for each other.

10. Each year the _____ of *Ramadan* _____ backward eleven days on the Roman calendar because the *Muslim* holidays are _____ on the lunar _____ .

© Instructional Fair • TS Denison

IF8728 Challenge Your Mind

Celebrating the New Life

Name _____

Spring

Different cultures around the world have unique ways of celebrating the newness of springtime. For many people spring means the beginning of the new year. Depending on the cultural group this may begin sometime between late January and early May. Use the code to translate the words into readable English.

1. the Iranian spring festival _____

2. in Iran, each family member would jump this to ask for a good luck blessing _____

3. the Iranian festival lasts this many days _____

4. the Thai water festival marking the start of the Buddhist new year _____

5. this is sprayed over crowds by enormous statues of Buddah _____

6. until 1752 this holiday was celebrated on March 25 in England _____

7. a "stinking idol" to the Puritans _____

8. on this day Christians celebrate victory of life over death _____

9. Vietnamese new year festival _____

10. legendary beast of good fortune in Vietnam _____

11. at this festival Vietnamese pay respect to these people _____

12. it celebrates Hebrew freedom from slavery _____

© Instructional Fair • TS Denison

IF8728 *Challenge Your Mind*

When a Girl Saved Her People

name _____

During Purim, Jews around the world recall how Esther, a beautiful Jewish-girl-turned-Persian queen, protected her people from annihilation. Her uncle Mordecai had once saved King Xerxes' life by uncovering a plot to assassinate the monarch. For this, Xerxes richly rewarded the uncle. The evil noble Haman in jealous hatred wanted Mordecai killed. He persuaded the monarch to pass an edict which called for the execution of all Jews in the empire. However, the brave princess, at a private banquet for the king and Haman, spoiled the cruel lord's plans when she informed them both that she too was a Jew. Haman was hung from the gallows he erected for Mordecai, and the Jewish citizens living in Persia did not die.

Unscramble the letters below to match each definition given.

Definition	Scrambled Letters	Answer
1. place of hangings	WOGLASL	_____
2. a law	DETIC	_____
3. a king	NMAHORC	_____
4. a special dinner	TAQENBU	_____
5. to remember	LACERL	_____
6. to murder a famous person	SNASIESTASA	_____
7. former name of Iran	SPAIRE	_____
8. to be covetous	SUOLAJE	_____
9. to ruin	LOPIS	_____
10. father's brother	NLECU	_____
11. destruction	LINIHOITANNA	_____
12. to convince	UREAPEDS	_____

© Instructional Fair • TS Denison

IF8728 Challenge Your Mind

Rock-A-Bye

name _____

The Doll's Festival

Fit the letters in each column into the boxes directly above them to form words. The letters may or may not go into the boxes in the same order in which they are given. Your finished puzzle will show a lullaby for a baby taken from a poem by Sir Walter Scott.

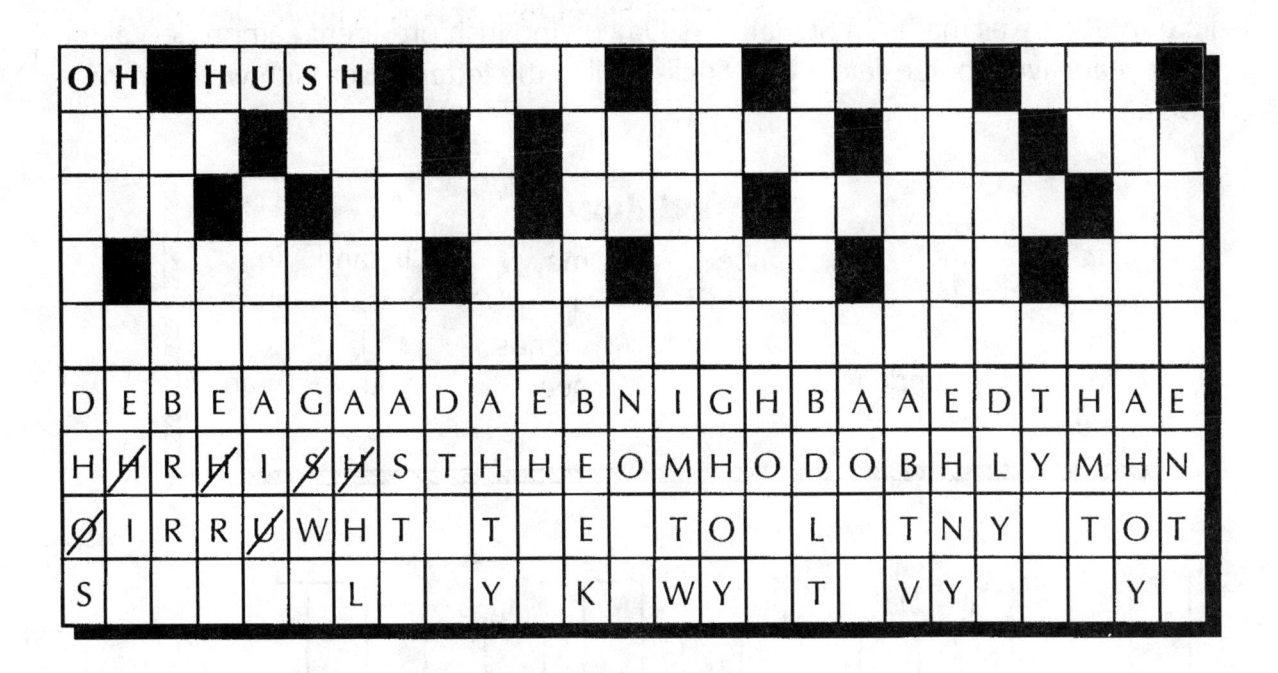

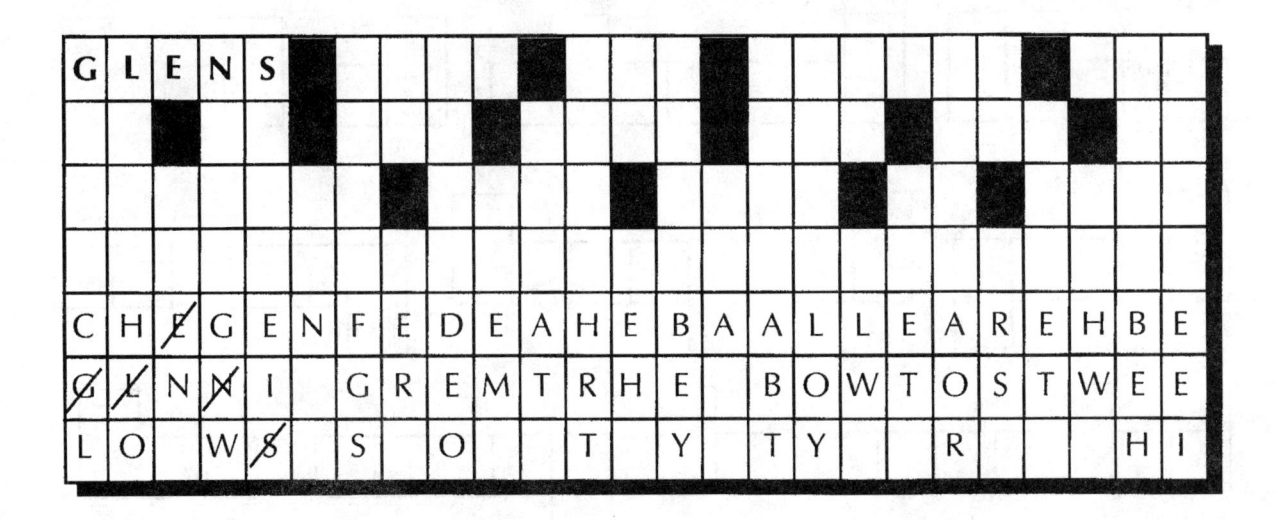

O	H		H	U	S	H																							

D	E	B	E	A	G	A	A	D	A	E	B	N	I	G	H	B	A	A	E	D	T	H	A	E
H	R	R	I	S	T	H	H	E	O	M	H	O	D	O	B	H	L	Y	M	H	N
I	R	R	W	H	T		T		E		T	O		L		T	N	Y		T	O	T
S				L		Y		K		W	Y		T		V	Y				Y

| G | L | E | N | S | | | | | | | | | | | | | | | | | | | | |

C	H	G	E	N	F	E	D	E	A	H	E	B	A	A	L	L	E	A	R	E	H	B	E
L	N	I		G	R	E	M	T	R	H	E		B	O	W	T	O	S	T	W	E	E
L	O	W		S		O		T		Y		T	Y				R				H	I

HELPFUL HINTS: Sir Walter Scott would have used an old English spelling for baby, but we used a contemporary spelling. Some words may wrap to a second line.

© Instructional Fair • TS Denison

IF8728 Challenge Your Mind

Go Gaelic!

name _____

Ar choimri' De' go raibh gach duine da'r gcairde agus sonas go dtuga Se' go fial do'ibhsean agus du'inne in Eirinn.

This Gaelic quotation was made on St. Patrick's Day by the Irish president Eamon de Valera more than 30 years ago. To translate it into English, fill in the letter boxes with words from the Word Box.

Word Box

an	and	be	may	Ireland	in
you	He	old	us	wish	in
of	I	would	friends	and	to
to	abundance	God's	peace	you	grant
care	here				

Th' Luck o' the Irish

Name _____

St. Patrick's Day

Decipher the names of these Saint Paddy's Day terms. The first letter of each object pictured is the letter that is written on each line.

1. _ _ _ _ _

2. _ _ _ _ _ _ _ _

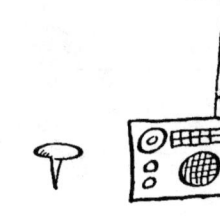

3. _ _ _ _ _ _

4. _ _ _ _ _ _ _ _

5. _ _ _ _ _ _ _ _ _ _

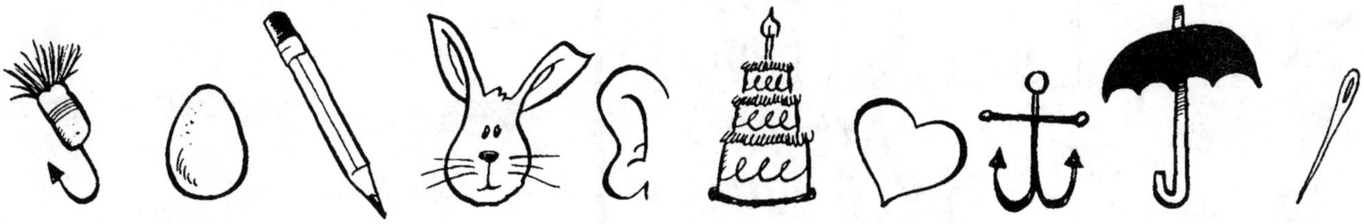

Challenge—Now design your own picture puzzles for these five terms:

Gaelic   Potato Famine   Limerick   Independence   James Joyce

The Wearin' o' the Green

Name _____

St. Patrick's Day

Provide words which match the descriptions below. Then read them in order from top to bottom. Use the first letter of each answer to find a word associated with Irish folklore. Need clues? Unscramble the words at the bottom of the page for the answers.

1. _____
2. _____
3. _____
4. _____
5. _____
6. _____
7. _____
8. _____
9. _____
10. _____

1. a silly 5-line poem
2. the land east of Ireland
3. _____ of gold
4. colorful display during or after a sun-sparkling rain shower
5. green gem
6. lucky sign: a 4-leafed _____
7. special day
8. poisonous snake
9. joined for a common cause
10. a grand lord

MOST OF IRELAND LIES 500 FEET ABOVE SEA LEVEL! AYE AND BEGORRAH!

Clues

pas	opt	lahiyod
verlco	boenl	deelamr
ceiiklmr	gdennla	abwrino
etnidu		

© Instructional Fair • TS Denison

IF8728 Challenge Your Mind

Rite of Spring or Stravinsky's Revenge

All the words in this cryptic puzzle follow the same code. A set of letters has been substituted for the correct letters of each word. These words relate to the topic *Spring*. Can you figure them out?

1. P C W X — BUDS
2. V Y T O J K — WARMTH
3. R G X U I J X — INSECTS
4. X K Q V U T X — SHOWERS
5. O Q V R G S — MOWING
6. A E Q V U T X — FLOWERS
7. P R T W X Q G S — BIRDSONG
8. H E Y G J R G S — PLANTING
9. U S S X — EGGS
10. S T U U G — GREEN
11. P E Q X X Q O X — BLOSSOMS
12. P R T J K — BIRTH
13. T Q P R G X — ROBINS
14. X U U W X — SEEDS
15. X C G X K R G U — SUNSHINE

CLUES:
1. The letter X represents S.
2. The letter Q represents O.
3. The letter S represents G.
4. The letter G represents N.

IGOR STRAVINSKY WAS A LAW STUDENT BEFORE HE BEGAN TO STUDY MUSICAL COMPOSITION!

Spring Madness

Three girls and two boys, ages 9 to 14, each perform some activity on this special religious holiday weekend. See if you can match each one with his or her age and activity.

Clues:

1. The ten-year-old girl, Ogden, and the person who seeds the flower bed are three different people.
2. The boy who goes to Mass is younger than Mary.
3. The eldest student bought new clothes for this holiday.
4. Petra is younger than the female who plants seeds. The girl who plants seeds is younger than Ogden.
5. Leo, who is not the nine-year-old egg-painter, is younger than 12 but older than Petra.
6. Nadia, who did not celebrate Passover, is not 12.
7. The youngest student is not Petra and does not celebrate Passover.

	celebrates Passover	seeds flower bed	buys clothes	attends Mass	paints Easter eggs	9	10	11	12	14
Leo										
Mary										
Nadia										
Ogden										
Petra										

PETRA WAS THE CAPITAL OF NABATAEA FROM 400 B.C. TO A.D. 200. REALLY!

Easter Words

Name _____

Write the words in the Word List next to the synonyms they match.

Word List	Related Words	Matching Word
cross	charity, mercy, leniency	_____
spring	animate, vital, existing	_____
grave	cottontail, hare	_____
flower	vernal, seedtime	_____
green	vault, hurdle, jump	_____
smile	amazement, marveling	_____
leap	beam, grin	_____
miracle	blossom, floret, bloom	_____
rabbit	crucifix	_____
grow	phenomenon, wonderment	_____
alive	propagate, cultivate, produce	_____
burst	tomb, mausoleum, crypt	_____
grace	ascent, mount	_____
wonder	verdant, fresh, new	_____
arise	flourish, explode	_____

© Instructional Fair • TS Denison

IF8728 Challenge Your Mind

Homophonic Homily

name _____

Easter

Complete the Easter story with words from the word list. As you determine each word, place it in the crossword. Use each word only once.

Word Pair List

altar/alter hair/hare
brake/break knew/new
feat/feet rite/write
grate/great threw/through
groan/grown watt/what

Believe it or not, one day we had to _____ (1) for a four-foot-tall white rabbit carrying an Easter basket. His name was Harvey. As he thanked us for avoiding his demise, Harvey showed us his _____ (2) big basket filled with chocolates, eggs, and various objects of springtime affection. Then he told us his story.

One Easter I foolishly fought with my sister Harmony. On that day long ago I _____ (3) four painted eggs at her. But not all of the eggs would _____ (4). No, indeed! I missed with three finely painted eggs which slipped through a _____ (5) in the street in front of our house. I was filled with remorse. My parents would scold me for hitting my sister, and I lost three of our precious creations. Loudly did I _____ (6) for I _____ (7) I would never see these eggs again. As Harmony tried to comb the eggy mess out of her _____ (8) she wailed, "_____ (9) have you done? You are a mean-spirited monster of a _____ (10)!" Then she scurried off to our warren to _____ (11) her appearance.

I remained outdoors, afraid to pass before my parents. As I stalled the arrival of my certain punishment, I saw movement behind the grate. I peeked _____ (12) the metal frame. Oh, I had _____ (13) much the past winter, and I needed to squeeze to enter the sewer. Down the line I saw a dim light. A 40-_____ (14) bulb was suspended from a wall. Before an _____ (15) made of stone and pebble stood an aged groundhog. He appeared to be performing some strange _____ (16) of spring. A _____ (17) brilliantly flowered Easter hat sat on his wide furry head. He solemnly turned toward me and said, "Be sure to _____ (18) about all you see here."

But this, alas, is too great a _____ (19) for one of my folk. I have never written with my fore-_____. (20)

HAY, WATT'S GNU?

© Instructional Fair • TS Denison

IF8728 Challenge Your Mind

Whiz-Dumb?

name _____

April Fools' Day

Fit the letters in each column into the boxes directly above them to form words. The letters may or may not go into the boxes in the same order in which they are given. Your completed puzzle is a proverb for this day. The first word is done for you.

	I	T											
O	S	L	I	E	H	T	A	A	L	D	E	E	I	H
I	O	O̸	L	I	N	O	R	B	W	C	E	S		N
I̸		I		W	S	O		H	N	I	S	S		F
		S		G	N				I	I	S			

I'M A LITTLE CONFUSED!

Hint: Some words may wrap to a second line.

Treed Me Right!

Name _____

Arbor Day

On Arbor Day many people make a habit of planting a tree. Can you plant a tree in your mind? Use the letter diagrams to name 25 trees.

Code:
A B C	J K L	T	X
D E F	M N O	S U	W Y
G H I	P Q R	V	Z

1. _____
2. _____
3. _____
4. _____
5. _____
6. _____
7. _____
8. _____
9. _____
10. _____
11. _____
12. _____
13. _____
14. _____
15. _____
16. _____
17. _____
18. _____
19. _____
20. _____
21. _____

A Toast to Critters

Name _____

Determine as many words as you can in the *Words* column. Then transfer these letters onto the *Solution* blanks with the same number code. You will have a poem by E.V. Rieu.

Definitions	Words
a large oceanic mammal	___ ___ ___ ___ ___ 1 2 3 4 5
an enormous American reptile; luggage skin	___ ___ ___ ___ ___ ___ ___ ___ ___ 6 7 8 9 10 11 12 13 14
an African ape that climbs well	___ ___ ___ ___ ___ ___ ___ ___ ___ ___ 15 16 17 18 19 20 21 22 23 24
a nocturnal, winged insect that produces its own light.	___ ___ ___ ___ ___ ___ ___ 25 26 27 28 29 30 31
a waterfowl of Donald fame	___ ___ ___ ___ 32 33 34 35
a great, antlered mammal of the North American forest	___ ___ ___ ___ ___ 36 37 38 39 40

Solution:

___ ___ ___ ___ ___ ___ ___ ___ ___ ___ ___ ___ ___ ___ ___ ___ ___ ___ ___ ___ ___ ___ ___ ___ ___
12 16 5   2 6 19 19 9 21 23 39 39   38 29 16 23 32 10 24 2 13 10 39

___ ___ ___ ___ ___ ___ ___ ___ ___ ___ ___ ___ ___ ___ ___ ___ ___ ___ ___. ___ ___ ___ ___
 8 26 24 39   9 21   15 13 36 19 4 5 12 40   27 40 19 13 39 24   12 2 40 31

___ ___ ___ ___ ___ ___ ___ ___ ___ ___ ___ ___ ___ ___ ___ ___ ___ ___ ___ ___ ___ ___ ___ ___
39 19 23 21 32   12 16 5   18 38 21 12 2 39 37   29 1 26 21 12 40 14   17 21

___ ___ ___ ___ ___ ___ ___ ___ ___ ___ ___ ___ ___ ___ ___ ___ ___ ___ ___ ___; ___ ___ ___ ___ ___
 3   8 13 21 10   32 28 7 26 34 17 37 33 39   32 37 22 5   20 21 32 26 25

___ ___ ___ ___ ___ ___ ___ ___ ___ ___ ___ ___ ___ ___ ___ ___ ___ ___ ___ ___ ___ ___ ___ ___ ___ ___ ___ ___ ___
12 16 28 31   21 13 12 24   12 16 40   12 17 18 24   11 12   6 30 7 12 16 24 31

"___ ___ ___ ___ ___ ___ ___ ___ ___ ___ ___ ___ ___ ___ ___ ___ ___ ___ ___ ___ ___ ___ ___!"
12 2 17 21 35   2 38 1   25 20 39 12 26 12   10 37   23 39

Giving to Caesar

name _____

Tax Day

Who says this is a holiday? Probably not adults. But if you play it right, you may be able to convince your folks to go out to eat . . . just to celebrate the completion of their taxes.

Find the List Words in the wordsearch below. The six unused letters in the puzzle will spell out a word in the end.

List Words

tax return	above
income	cash
deduction	gift
benefit	call
family	busy
bond	local
residence	interest
send	limit
self	join
land	loser
note	status
amount	home
refund	social security
late	adjustment
federal	real estate
less	revenue
pain	internal
cent	exempt
report	joint
nervous	item
alien	

E	E	P	A	E	X	E	M	P	T	Y	L
C	P	T	N	E	M	O	C	N	I	Y	A
N	R	A	O	Y	L	I	M	A	F	T	C
E	E	X	I	N	E	A	E	S	E	I	O
D	A	R	T	N	S	M	U	T	N	R	L
I	L	E	C	D	S	O	N	A	E	U	I
S	E	T	U	E	V	U	E	T	B	C	M
E	S	U	D	R	N	N	V	U	U	E	I
R	T	R	E	L	A	T	E	S	S	S	T
L	A	N	D	N	O	B	R	A	Y	L	S
S	T	N	E	M	T	S	U	J	D	A	E
H	E	I	L	A	N	R	E	T	N	I	R
S	L	L	I	T	I	V	O	R	U	C	E
A	A	T	F	H	O	M	E	P	F	O	T
C	E	I	Y	B	J	O	I	N	E	S	N
M	G	L	A	R	E	D	E	F	R	R	I

___ ___ ___ ___ ___ ___

TAXATION WAS ONE OF THE MAIN CAUSES OF THE REVOLUTIONARY WAR!

© Instructional Fair • TS Denison

IF8728 Challenge Your Mind

On to Lexington!

Name _____

Patriot Day

This day is celebrated especially in parts of Massachusetts and Maine. It honors patriots of the American Revolution. Use the Letter List to add a letter to each word. Then rearrange the letters to form words about the patriots.

Letter List
C C C C E H H K N N O R R R R S T T T X

WORD	Letter	New Word	Hint
1. boost	___	_____	MA city
2. slider	___	_____	redcoat
3. lives	___	_____	precious metals
4. die	___	_____	to be carried along
5. rental	___	_____	old light
6. sore	___	_____	mare or filly
7. loony	___	_____	one of 13
8. real	___	_____	to warn
9. bleat	___	_____	larger than a skirmish
10. rot	___	_____	British loyalist
11. cordon	___	_____	town of early battle
12. mutes	___	_____	old-fashioned gun
13. harm	___	_____	military walk
14. pasture	___	_____	seizes
15. arbor	___	_____	port
16. sort	___	_____	prances
17. thou	___	_____	yell
18. sine	___	_____	straps of a horse's bit
19. lathe	___	_____	horse's lead rope
20. teas	___	_____	money for the IRS

© Instructional Fair • TS Denison

IF8728 Challenge Your Mind

All Is Mended

Shakespeare's Birthday

name _____

Below are quotes from five of William Shakespeare's great plays. Unscramble the name of each speaker and fill in the name of each play. May the world be your stage.

1. The pound of flesh which I demand of him
   Is dearly bought, is mine, and I will have it. (IV.i.99)   c h k l o s y _____

   Play: e t h   a n c r e m h t   f o   i c n v e e   ___ ___ ___   ___ ___ ___ ___ ___ ___ ___ ___   ___ ___   ___ ___ ___ ___ ___ ___

2. When we are born, we cry that we are come
   To this great stage of fools. (IV.vi.182-183)   a e l r _____

   Play: a i n r l g k e   ___ ___ ___ ___   ___ ___ ___

3. My hour is almost come,
   When I to sulf'rous and tormenting flames
   Must render up myself. (I.iv. 3-5)   t s o h g _____

   Play: l e m h a t   ___ ___ ___ ___ ___ ___

4. If we shadows have offended,
   Think but this, and all is mended:
   That you have but slumb'red here,
   While these visions did appear. (V.i. 422-425)   c u p k _____

   Play: a   m d s u m r e i m   s i h t g n   a e m r d   ___   ___ ___ ___ ___ ___ ___ ___ ___ ___   ___ ___ ___ ___ ___ ___   ___ ___ ___ ___ ___

5. The more my wrong, the more his spite appears.
   What, did he marry me to famish me? (IV.iii. 2-3)   a e k t _____

   Play: e h t   g i a m t n   f o   e t h   w e h r s   ___ ___ ___   ___ ___ ___ ___ ___ ___   ___ ___   ___ ___ ___   ___ ___ ___ ___ ___

Speakers

ghost   Shylock
Puck   Kate
Lear

Titles

- A Midsummer Night's Dream
- Anthony and Cleopatra
- The Merchant of Venice
- The Taming of the Shrew
- Hamlet
- Henry IV
- King Lear
- Romeo and Juliet
- Othello

Bow to the Bard

name _____

Shakespeare's Birthday

Fit the letters of each column into the boxes directly above them to form words. The letters may or may not go into the boxes in the same order in which they are given. The finished puzzle will give the names of seven of William Shakespeare's plays.

SHAKESPEARE WROTE 36 PLAYS, 154 SONNETS AND 2 NARRATIVE POEMS!

I BET HIS HAND WAS TIRED!

T	H	E	★								★		★								■		
			■					★			■				★							■	
					★		★						■		★								
★						★				■							★						
	J̶	J̶		A	N			A	E	A		E	J		A		M	S		C	A	E	M	A	R
L	N	E	G	H	E	N	C		R	E	A	I	O	T	H	E		N	I	C	E	E	M	S	E	R
O	L	I	O	K	I	R	D	D	J	N	T	M		F	U	L	E	U	I	D		P	U	O	T	H	R
J̶	M	O		M	T	S	G	H	L	U	L	R		T		V	I	T	E	M	S		S	T		E

Title List

Julius Caesar
Romeo and Juliet
The Tempest
Othello

King Lear
The Merchant of Venice
A Midsummer Night's Dream

Hint: Some words may wrap to a second line.

© Instructional Fair • TS Denison

IF8728 *Challenge Your Mind*

Singing Sweetly (Sometimes)

name _____

Bird Day

Fill in the boxes below with the names of birds. Use lowercase letters as you write.

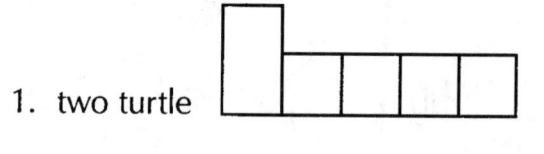

1. two turtle
2. Jonathan Livingston
3. Mother
4. Baltimore
5. __ , __ , in and out my window
6. Woody
7. _____ clock
8. _____ Little
9. _____ redbreast

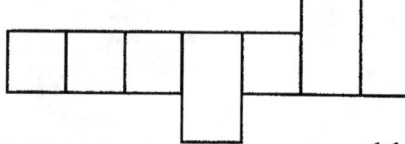

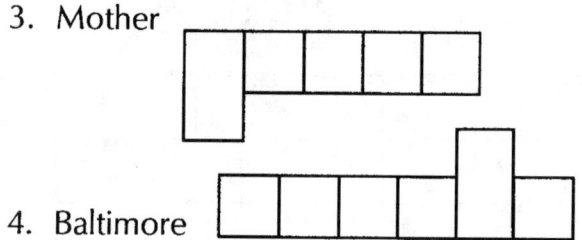

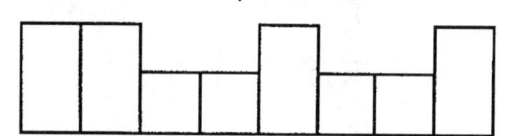

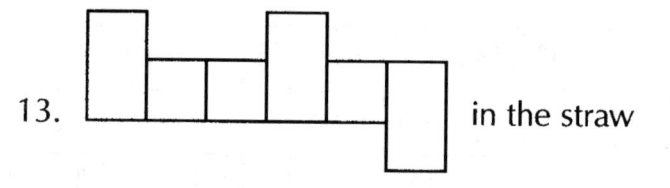

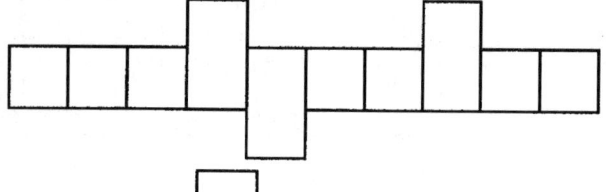

10. wise old
11. listen to the . . .
12. crazy as a
13. _____ in the straw
14. the ___ brings the baby
15. fly like an
16. _____ -toed
17. eyes like a ____

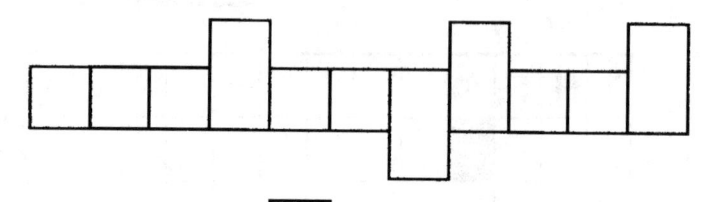

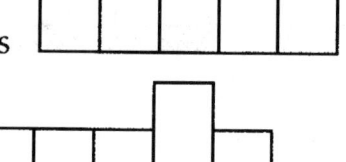

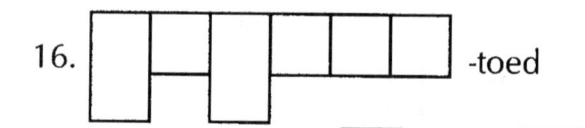

Hail, Bounteous May!

Name _____

May Day celebrates flowers with a dance around the Maypole using festoons of ribbon. Its tradition, though old, is not as common today in the United States and Canada.

Match the words from the Word Box with their synonyms. Write the words in the boxes provided.

_____	_____	_____
bemask cloak dissimulate	caper romp frisk	adolescence greenness juvenility

_____	_____	_____
ardor zeal fervor	exaltation euphoria inspiration	vault spring hurdle

_____	_____	_____
pep dash oomph	suitable qualified worthy	blithe sprightly carefree

_____	_____	_____
coquettish coy playful	crow jubilate triumph	garnish bedeck trim

_____	_____	_____
savor treasure cherish	recreation sport disport	unblemished pure blameless

Word Box: adorn, appreciate, disguise, elation, eligible, enthusiasm, exult, flirtatious, gambol, innocent, jump, lighthearted, play, spirit, youth

Birthday for Buddha

name _____

Wesak

Place the letters in each column in the boxes directly above them to form words. The letters may or may not go in the boxes in the same order in which they are given. Your finished puzzle will give part of the Buddha story.

| W | H | E | N | | | | | | | | | | | | | | | | | | | | |

D	A	B	E	E	B	A	D	D	H	A	A	H	A	A	A	B	E	D	A	I	A	A
E	~~H~~	~~L~~	H	H	O	E	D	D	H	D		H	D	A	O	B	N	R	E	N	D	E
M	P	O	I	L	T	U	N	R	L	E		H	E	N	V	E	N	S	N	O	H	E
~~W~~		R	~~N~~	N		W	O	T	T	O		I	E	S	V	E	O	V			N	N
		T	T			W							S		W	O			R	O		

Hint: Some words may wrap to a second line.

BUDDHA MEANS ENLIGHTENED ONE!

Mom and Me

Name _____

Mother's Day

In honor of all mothers in the world, enjoy this poem by Ogden Nash entitled "The Guppy." Place the letters in each column in the boxes directly above them to form words. The letters may or may not go in the boxes in the same order in which they are given.

[Fallen-letter puzzle grid with "WHALES" filled in at top left and "B" at upper right]

Speech bubble: OGDEN NASH ALSO COLLABORATED ON THE 1943 MUSICAL "ONE TOUCH OF VENUS"...IT WAS A BIG HIT!

Hint: Some words may wrap to a second line.

© Instructional Fair • TS Denison

IF8728 Challenge Your Mind

Words Cannot Describe (but I'll try)

name _____

Mother's Day

Fill in this chart using words that begin with the letters shown at the top of each column. Find as many as you can. You may use information sources to help your search. Have 2 or 3 others complete charts too. Then compare your answers crossing out any duplicates. See which person has the most items unmarked.

Category	A	D	O	R	E
Famous women (last names)					
Verbs that show a mother's actions					
Occupations					
Flowers or trees your mother might give you					

© Instructional Fair • TS Denison

IF8728 *Challenge Your Mind*

The Lady with the Lamp

Name _____

Florence Nightingale's Birthday

May 12 is the birthdate of Florence Nightingale, a person important to hospital reforms of the 19th and 20th centuries. Use the clues to scramble and add one letter to each word to form a new word associated with the work and life of Florence Nightingale.

Letters to be added include:

d d h l l m m n o o r r u y y

#	Word	Letter	New Word	Hint
1.	those	___	_____	to calm, relieve, or pacify
2.	down	___	_____	an injury
3.	pal	___	_____	instrument of light
4.	saw	___	_____	skirmishes where Nightingale aided
5.	dice	___	_____	a physician
6.	places	___	_____	a cutting tool in surgery
7.	bold	___	_____	life fluid
8.	vase	___	_____	a healing ointment
9.	sure	___	_____	one who cares for the sick
10.	ale	___	_____	to recover, to restore the body
11.	heat	___	_____	the sorrow of war
12.	scorers	___	_____	a world health agency
13.	licks	___	_____	ill, unhealthy
14.	yam	___	_____	a military unit
15.	tail	___	_____	Nightingale's birth country, like a boot

SHE WAS THE FIRST WOMAN AWARDED THE BRITISH ORDER OF MERIT!

© Instructional Fair • TS Denison

IF8728 *Challenge Your Mind*

We Salute You!

name _____

Memorial Day

This holiday celebration was begun after the Civil War to honor those who died for our nation, both North and South.

Find the 5-letter words by the process of elimination and deduction. Fill in the blanks with five-letter answers to each definition. The number in parentheses tells how many of the letters in the answer are also in each Memorial Day clue word. The boxes tell you the correct position(s). The first one is done for you.

clue word	H	O	N	O	R	
to burn with hot liquid	s	c	a	l	d	(0)
to experience with pleasure	_	☐	_	☐	_	(2)
aircraft *driver*	_	_	_	☐	_	(1)
wails or cries like a baby	_	_	_	_	_	(0)
very hot vapor	_	_	_	_	_	(0)
stallion, for example	☐	☐	☐	_	_	(3)
cocoa-colored, for example	_	☐	☐	_	☐	(3)
listened	☐	_	_	☐	_	(2)
instruments for doing work	_	☐	☐	_	_	(2)

clue word	G	R	A	V	E	
to expell	☐	☐	_	_	_	(2)
horizontal ledge	_	_	☐	_	_	(1)
tongue of fire	_	_	☐	_	☐	(2)
deep, angry, dog noise	☐	☐	_	_	_	(2)
wooly, fluffy	_	_	_	_	_	(0)
hazy; unspecific	☐	☐	☐	_	☐	(4)
a small riot	_	☐	☐	_	_	(2)
having much foliage	_	☐	☐	_	_	(2)
the entire amount, all	_	_	_	_	☐	(1)

© Instructional Fair • TS Denison

(44)

IF8728 *Challenge Your Mind*

We Remember

name _____

Memorial Day

Find 31 words related to Memorial Day in this wordsearch.

Word Bank

ballgame	duty	ham	memorial	serve
bands	family	home	Monday	speeches
barbecue	flag	honor	parades	swim
bell	grill	horseshoes	picnic	uniform
camping	graves	march	remember	veterans
cemetery	gun	May	sad	waving
drum				

C	E	M	Y	R	E	M	E	M	B	E	R	C	B
I	V	E	T	E	R	A	N	S	C	M	M	S	A
N	R	M	U	S	W	I	M	P	A	A	R	E	R
C	E	O	D	A	S	A	A	E	M	G	O	O	B
I	S	R	V	D	H	R	F	E	P	L	F	H	E
P	U	I	N	H	A	O	A	C	I	L	I	S	C
M	N	A	H	D	A	N	M	H	N	A	N	E	U
G	B	L	E	C	U	O	I	E	G	B	U	S	E
A	E	S	O	G	R	H	L	S	E	V	A	R	G
L	L	I	R	G	M	A	Y	Y	A	D	N	O	M
F	L	Y	R	E	T	E	M	E	C	D	S	H	L

MEMORIAL DAY WAS FIRST WIDELY OBSERVED ON MAY 30, 1868!

Extra: How many words can you create using the letters in these words?

flowers for soldiers

© Instructional Fair • TS Denison

IF8728 Challenge Your Mind

The Picture-esque Americas

Pan American Day

name _____

Figure out the names of these countries of the Americas. Each picture represents a letter of the alphabet. Note that some letters may be represented by more than one picture symbol.

1. _ _ _ _ _ _

2. _ _ _ _ _

3. _ _ _ _ _ _

4. _ _ _ _ _ _ _

5. _ _ _ _ _ _

6. _ _ _ _ _

Now design your own picture puzzles for these four countries:

Costa Rica   Argentina   Honduras   Brazil

© Instructional Fair • TS Denison   IF8728 Challenge Your Mind

Wave Your Flag High

name _____

Flag Day

To complete this page rearrange the letters to form the name of a Canadian province or U.S. state. Your completed puzzle will share a slogan true to each country.

1. This state flag shows a red **C** overlaying two blue stripes and one white horizontal stripe.
   O COLD OAR

2. This state flag shows a white palm tree and a crescent moon on a blue background.
   AN OIL CRUSH OAT

3. This provincial flag shows a square-sailed vessel with four oars.
   WIN WRECK BUNS

4. This state flag shows a yellow torch surrounded by 19 stars on a blue background.
   AIDA INN

5. This provincial flag shows the Union Jack in the upper left corner and a buffalo on a red background.
   BOAT MAIN

6. This state flag shows a bear, a red star, and a red stripe on a white background.
   IF ACORN AIL

7. This state flag shows a ceremonial Indian shield on a blue background.
   LO HAM OAK

8. This state flag shows three red, three white, and two blue horizontal stripes with a Union Jack in the upper left corner.
   AW I AH I

9. This state flag has two red stripes criss-crossing its white field.
   A BAA ALM

10. This provincial flag shows 4 white *fleurs-de-lis* surrounding a white cross on a blue background.
    BE CUE Q

11. This state flag has a copper-colored star from which red and yellow rays extend. The bottom half of the flag is blue.
    AN OZ AIR

12. This state flag shows three white stars in a blue circle on a red field. One blue stripe runs down the right-hand edge.
    SEEN TEENS

13. This state flag shows a white buffalo in a blue field with a white and red border.
    MY NOWIG

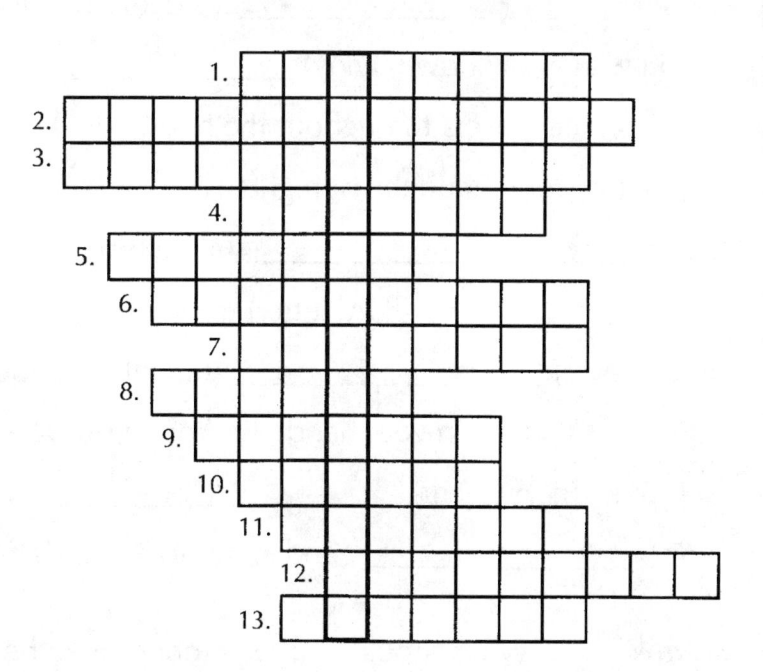

© Instructional Fair • TS Denison

IF8728 Challenge Your Mind

G'mornin', Poppa!

Name _____

Father's Day

Fill in the blanks below with synonyms of the words in parentheses. Then use the suggested letter from the replacement word to find the answer to the riddle.

Word Bank

assistive	jaunt	sagacious
cherish	leggings	shrewd
dexterous	mindless	slumber
engaged	pacifistic	vintage
globoid	rightful	windy

1. G'morning, Poppa! Oh, did I wake you? I just wanna say how much I (*appreciate*) _____ (2nd letter) you. 2. There's that (*distinctive*) _____ (1st letter) furrow above your eyes that makes you look so smart. 3. Oh, by the way, I gotcha these (*socks*) _____ (5th letter). I hope they fit. If not, I guess I'll hafta wear them myself. 4. And I just want you to know I was wrong to smash in the headlight and your discipline was (*just*) _____ (2nd letter). 5. I promise to be more (*helpful*) _____ (6th letter) next time I change the lightbulb in the garage. 6. It's too bad you were so (*busy*) _____ (1st letter) retrieving the golf balls that I putted into the street. 7. Yeah, Poppa, you were definitely (*wise*) _____ (3rd letter) to lock your golf clubs in your bedroom closet. 8. And I wanna say how (*handy*) _____ (4th letter) you are putting in all those locks on the closets throughout the house. 9. Did you (*sleep*) _____ (4th letter) long enough last night? 10. I guess my music at two in the morning was a bit (*thoughtless*) _____ (6th letter) of me, huh? 11. Do you think I'm a bit too (*talkative*) _____ (3rd letter) this morning? 12. Well, if you think so, you must be right. You're one (*clever*) _____ (6th letter) dude. 13. Hey, what's that (*round*) _____ (3rd letter) object in your hand? 14. You're not plannin' to throw that baseball at me, are you? But you're so (*nonviolent*) _____ (6th letter)! 15. . . . You're sending me on a (*trip*) _____ (2nd letter) to Aunt Mabel's in Cleveland. I'll miss you, Poppa!

Riddle: What should you remember for Father's Day?

___ ___ ___ ___   ___ ___ ___ ___   ___ ___ ___   ___ ___ ___ ___
12 13 11 5   7 4 2 10   1 14 9   15 8 3 6

© Instructional Fair • TS Denison   IF8728 *Challenge Your Mind*

Warm and Sunny

Name _____

First Day of Summer

Fill in the boxes with words for summer. Use lowercase letters as you write.

1. mound of a six-legged social crawler

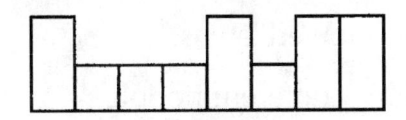

2. America's pastime

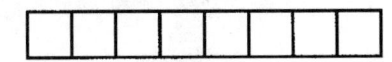

3. cool cone or bowl dessert

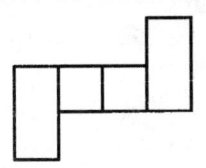

4. "in the _____ ol' summertime"

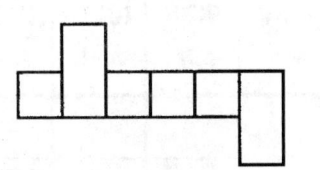

5. refreshing water sport _____

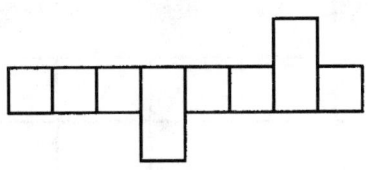

6. pesky blood-sucking insect

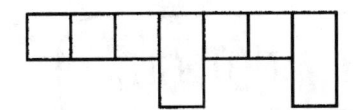

7. family outing in tent

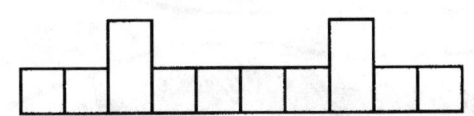

8. large, red-pulped fruit from a vine

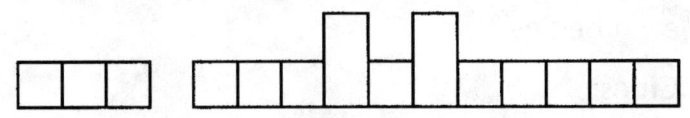

9. invention that cools room

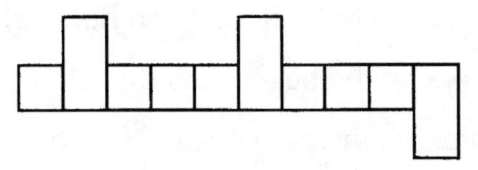

10. fruit with seeds on its "skin"

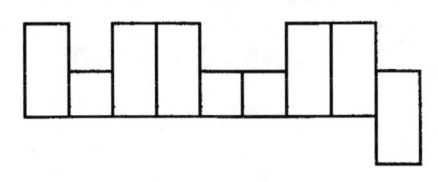

11. beautifully colored day creature

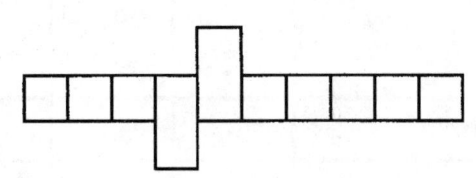

12. these protect the *blinkers* from old Sol

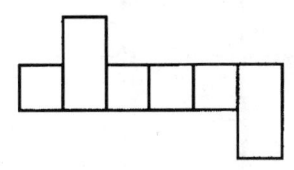

13. sweet or tart fruit of the season

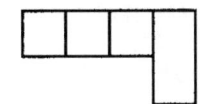

14. bee's stinging cousin

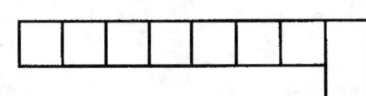

15. hot day exercise

© Instructional Fair • TS Denison

IF8728 Challenge Your Mind

A Simmerin' Summer

name _____

First Day of Summer

Annie and four friends celebrate the first day of summer in five different ways. Each begins his/her activities at a different time of the day. Use the matrix to find out what each one does and when each begins.

Clues:

1. Carrie, who didn't go on a picnic, isn't the girl who went to the pool at 10:30 A.M.
2. Ben began his activity at least two hours after the girl who mowed lawns.
3. Elsie, the one at the beach, and the 11:30 A.M. beginner are 3 different people.
4. The swimmer at the pool began after the mower but before the boy at the beach. None of these people began at 9:00 A.M.
5. Daryl is the dog walker.
6. The picnicker began after the one at the pool.

	mow grass	go to beach	swim in pool	walk dog	have picnic	9:00 A.M.	9:30 A.M.	10:30 A.M.	11:30 A.M.	1:00 P.M.
Annie										
Ben										
Carrie										
Daryl										
Elsie										

SORRY DUDE...I'M NOT OUT OF BED UNTIL NOON!

© Instructional Fair • TS Denison

IF8728 *Challenge Your Mind*

Overcoming Adversity

Name _____

Helen Keller's Birthday

Use the code to complete the quotation about Helen Keller. Follow the code row by row until all the blanks are filled in. Cross off each letter square as you use it. The first word has been done for you.

Code: 5 2 7 3 6 8 1 4

	1	2	3	4	5	6	7	8
	G̸	L̸	H̸	H̸	A̸	O̸	T̸	U̸
	E	L	N	A	B	D	I	D
	T	A	D	E	F	M	N	U
	C	U	T	H	D	O	E	A
	D	L	H	F	I	O	D	O
	L	V	R	E	E	H	E	E
	R	K	L	B	N	L	E	E
	W	C	M	O	E	E	A	A
	O	L	R	W	R	E	D	N
	H	E	A	O	N	U	D	T
	E	A	D	A	R	S	N	P
	A	E	T	Y	K	O	R	D
	L	E	E	L	W	C	R	A
	C	E	T	H	H	E	R	A
	S	R	N	U	E	N	A	E
	A	L	V	S	L	A	I	N
	A	H	M	C	T	I	E	R
	E	E	O	R	L	R	W	K

HELEN KELLER GRADUATED WITH HONORS FROM RADCLIFFE COLLEGE IN 1904!

$\underline{A}\ \underline{L}\ \underline{T}\ \underline{H}\ \underline{O}\ \underline{U}\ \underline{G}\ \underline{H}$ ___ ___ ___ ___, ___ ___ ___, ___ ___ ___
 5 2 7 3 6 8 1 4

___ ___ ___ ___ ___ ___ ___ ___ ___ ___

___ ___ ___ ___ ___, ___ ___ ___ — ___ ___ ___

___ ___ ___ ___ ___ ___ ___ ___ ___ ___ ___ ___ ___.

___ ___ ___ ___ ___ ___ ___ ___ ___ ___ ___ ___ ___,

___ ___ ___ ___ ___ ___ ___ ___ ___, " ___ ___ ___

___ ___ ___."

© Instructional Fair • TS Denison

IF8728 Challenge Your Mind

In Praise of Summer

name _____

Summer Vacation

Fit the letters in each column into the boxes directly above them to form words. The letters may or may not go into the boxes in the same order in which they are given. One word is done for you. Your finished puzzle may give you summer cheer. Enjoy your vacation!

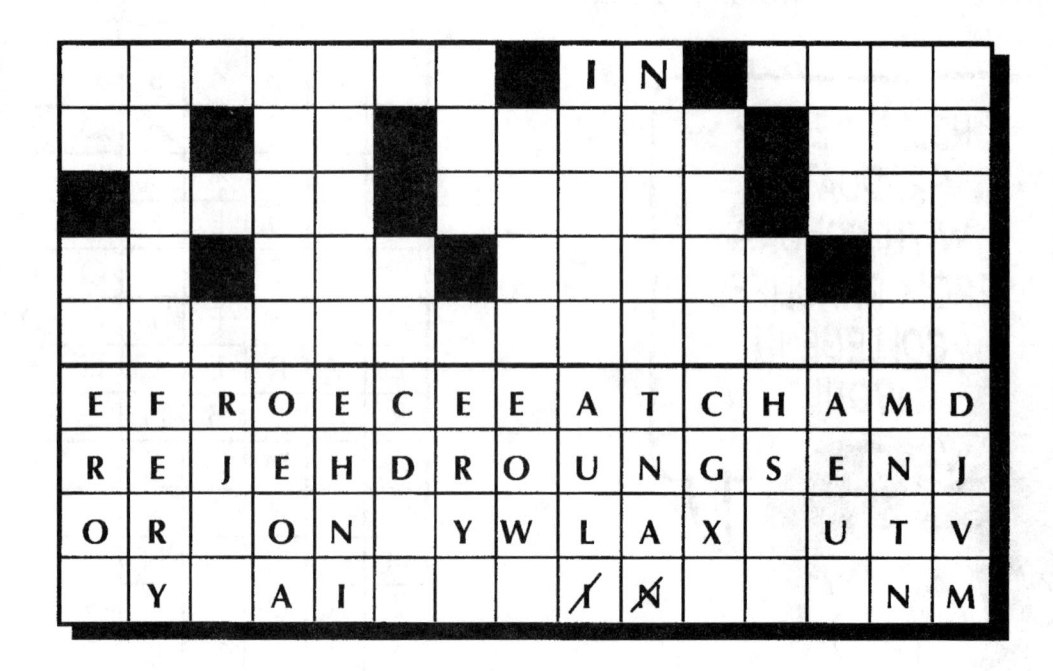

							I	N				
E	F	R	O	E	C	E	E	A	T	C	H	A	M	D
R	E	J	E	H	D	R	O	U	N	G	S	E	N	J
O	R		O	N		Y	W	L	A	X		U	T	V
	Y		A	I				̸L	̸N				N	M

I, LIKE, YOU KNOW, REALLY DIG SUMMER!

Hint: Some words may wrap to a second line.

The Great North Country

Name _____

Canada Day

Each entry is written in code. Use the clues to decode the mystery and name the terms.

Clue	Entry	Answer
1. Canada's capital city	DEERCR	_____
2. what this day honors, Canada's ____	QWLBVBWLBWZB	_____
3. country which once "owned" Canada	PNBRE GNQERQW	_____
4. Canada's government leader	VNQKB KQWQUEBN	_____
5. Canadian "state"	VNDSQWZB	_____
6. Canada is the world's largest country	UBZDWL	_____
7. because it's so wide, Canada has six ___	EQKB FDWBU	_____
8. its northern border	RNZEQZ DZBRW	_____
9. easternmost province	WBCYDJWLORWL	_____
10. city with annual stampede	ZROPRNT	_____
11. chief Pacific port	SRWZDJSBN	_____
12. famous Atlantic fishing site	PNRWL GRWHU	_____
13. watery highway to the interior	UE ORCNBWZB UBRCRT	_____
14. Albertan National Park	ARUVBN	_____
15. symbol of Canada	KRVOB OBRY	_____
16. smallest province	VNQWZB	_____
	BLCRNL	_____
	QUORWL	_____

Canada's Motto: YNDK UBR ED UBR

___ ___ ___ ___   ___ ___ ___   ___ ___   ___ ___ ___

CANADA'S NAME IS THOUGHT TO BE DERIVED FROM THE IROQUOIS WORD FOR COMMUNITY —KANATA!

You're a Grand Old Flag!

name _____

U.S. Independence Day

Fill in this chart using words that begin with the letters shown at the top of each column. Find as many as you can. You may use information sources to help your search. Have 2 or 3 others complete charts too. Then compare your answers, crossing out any that duplicate. See which person has the most items unmarked.

Category	F	L	A	G	S
American Patriots (First or Last Names)					
Sports, Games, and Other Activities					
Picnic Food					
Vacation Spots					

At the Bridge

name _____

U.S. Independence Day

On this date in 1837, Ralph Waldo Emerson dedicated a memorial near a bridge in Concord, Massachusetts.

Use the Word Box to help you fill in the diagram to learn what he said. The quotation will read from left to right and some words wrap to the next line. We have included letters for some of the words to assist you.

RALPH WALDO EMERSON ATTENDED HARVARD COLLEGE FROM 1817 TO 1821!

B	Y	T	H	E	R	U	D	E			D
G			A					E			
			O								F
		G				R					
		Z						D			
		T			F						
S											
			S					R			
	U				W						

Word Box

and	flood	the	bridge	round	world	stood
flag	the	breeze	once	unfurled	farmers	that
the	arched	here	to	embattled	shot	the
April's	heard	their	by	rude	fired	the

On This Day

name _____

Bastille Day

Use the Word Box to unscramble the garbled words to tell what this day commemorates.

This day marks the French (TOLANAIN) _____ holiday.
On this day the country of France (ERSCTEBEAL) _____ by setting off (SRRKAEFICCRE) _____ . The Bastille was an ancient (TOSFSERR) _____ in (IRSAP) _____ , but it had become a (SPINOR) _____ ,and many of the French people had grown to (SEEDSIP) _____ the structure. On July 14, 1789, as the French (TREINOOLVU) _____ began, an (YARNG) _____ crowd of people met outside the fortress and demanded the (STUNNIMOI) _____ stored inside. (YETVEALNUL) _____ the mob fought their way in and (TEDDYSORE) _____ the building.

Use the words you have written to complete the word puzzle.

Word Box

prison
eventually
national
despise
destroyed
fortress
angry
celebrates
Paris
munitions
revolution
firecrackers

B A S T I L L E D A Y

We All Scream for Ice Cream

name _____

National Ice Cream Day

Today is the day to enjoy this cool treat. Maybe you'll want to stay in the shade as you complete this word fill-in.

3 letters
icy

4 letters
bowl
cold
cone
foam
lick
soft

5 letters
dairy
peach
split
swell
swirl
tasty

6 letters
banana
frozen
malted
pecans
plenty
sundae
vanilla

7 letters
chatter
tin roof

8 letters
blue moon
snickers
Superman

9 letters
bubblegum
pistachio
raspberry
rocky road
chocolate

10 letters
strawberry

11 letters
cookie dough
moosetracks

15 letters
cookies and cream
cookies and fudge
peppermint stick

16 letters
marshmallow swirl
pralines and cream

17 letters
mint chocolate chip

19 letters
Mackinac Island fudge

20 letters
strawberry cheesecake

21 letters
chocolate peanutbutter

© Instructional Fair • TS Denison

IF8728 Challenge Your Mind

Lunar Madness

name _____

On July 20, 1969, American astronauts first landed on the moon. In honor of that event try this puzzle about the moon and space. Each word or phrase below can be changed to a word or phrase relating to the space program. Use the definition clues whenever you become stuck. Good luck!

Words	Space Phrase	Definition Clue
1. TRACER (1 word)	_____	a pit in the moon's surface
2. CAPES (1 word)	_____	"the final frontier"
3. HEALTH DIES (2 words)	_____	a protection against overheating upon re-entry
4. "LA LOOP" (1 word)	_____	the craft type used in 1969
5. NASA TROUT (1 word)	_____	American space traveler
6. REMOTE (1 word)	_____	a shooting star
7. ARMS (1 word)	_____	4th planet from the sun
8. DIET SOAR (1 word)	_____	"star shaped"
9. NEAR RIM (1 word)	_____	an early space satellite
10. THUS LET (1 word)	_____	space taxi service
11. MINOR BOOST (2 words)	_____	lunar circle around us
12. GLANDULAR INN (2 words)	_____	arrival on moon's surface
13. CLEFT NURSES (2 words)	_____	how moon shines in night
14. ASK BITTY LOANS (2 words)	_____	Earth's space platform
15. THE RAG VARSITY (2 words)	_____	what keeps us on Earth
16. MOTH MOAN NINE (4 words)	_____	what some claim they see when they view our satellite

Beware the Flute Player!   name _____

Use the Word Box to write synonyms of the bold-faced words.

A visiting musician **came to** _____ Hamelin Town as its townsfolk **suffered** _____ an infestation of rats. The rats were causing a **horrid** _____ health **hazard** _____ , that was killing many people. The numbers and fearlessness of these **marauding** _____ rodents terrified the folk of Hamelin.

For whatever reason of his own, the town visitor **suggested** _____ that he take responsibility for **driving** _____ the vermin from the city. He asked an **exorbitant** _____ fee to which the town council members gave false **pledge** _____ of payment. After he rid the town of its rats, playing his flute before the **packs** _____ , the pied-cloaked piper was denied **payment** _____ . We can well imagine his **seething** _____ anger.

While records are slim in detail, we do know that the children of Hamelin vanished at **roughly** _____ the same time as the unpaid piper. One **story** _____ claims that the children all suffered some **mysterious** _____ malady. The music-making flautist led the **wan** _____ children from the city while their parents prayed in the town's church. Were the children sold as slaves? Did they all **die** _____ in the forest? We can only **guess** _____ . Yet a stained-glass window in the ancient Hamelin church **shows** _____ a pied-cloaked piper, a rat, and a **child** _____ .

Word Box

about	danger	excessive	propelling	surmise
awful	depicts	pale	puzzling	swarms
boiling	endured	promise	raiding	tale
compensation	entered	proposed	succumb	youngster

Brother and Sister

name _____

Raksha Bandhan

This Hindu holiday honors brothers and sisters. Girls and women tie bracelets around the arms of their brothers who, in turn, promise to care for them. Use the clues below to match each brother and sister, identifying the color of each one's bracelet and the protection promised by each brother.

Clues:

1. Kacia, whose brother is not Lal, gave a blue bracelet. Zail did not receive this blue bracelet.
2. The brother who promised to protect his sister from dogs (not Kim) received a green bracelet.
3. Kim, who either received a gold or a red bracelet, promised to protect his sister from strangers.
4. Leema, who is promised protection from bullies, has no brother named Kim or Zail.
5. Indira's brother has a green bracelet. Shanda did not tie a gold bracelet around her brother's arm.

		Indira	Kacia	Leema	Shanda	bully	dark	dogs	strangers	blue	gold	green	red
Brother	Kim												
	Lal												
	Rajiv												
	Zail												
Color of Bracelet	blue								
	gold								
	green								
	red								
Protect From	bully				
	dark				
	dogs				
	strangers				

HINDUISM IS THE MAJOR RELIGION OF INDIA!

© Instructional Fair • TS Denison

IF8728 Challenge Your Mind

The Flash

Name _____

Hiroshima Day

On this day in 1945, the United States unleashed the atomic bomb on the city of Hiroshima. The immediate and following chaos shocked both the Japanese and the Allied nations. Nine days later the Japanese surrendered.

Match a word from the Word Box to its definition. The letter boxes may help you do this more easily.

Word Box

Atomic Bomb Dome	Hirohito	mushroom	Oppenheimer
Enola Gay	Honshu	Nagasaki	Ota River
fallout	Japan	nuclear weapon	Peace Memorial Park
genocide	Manahattan Project	O-Bon Festival	radiation sickness

1. a day to honor one's ancestors

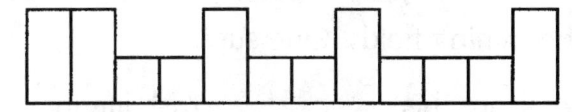

2. the plan for developing a nuclear weapon

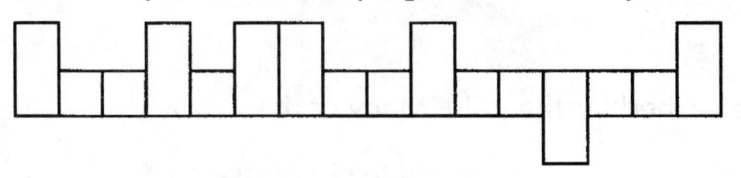

3. the physicist who contributed most to develop the atomic bomb

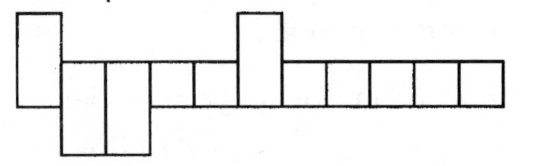

4. seven tributaries feed this waterway at Hiroshima

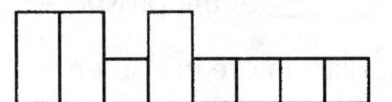

5. the shape of the after-flash cloud

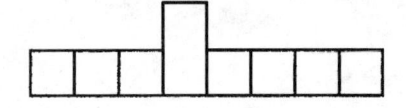

6. the emperor of Japan in 1945

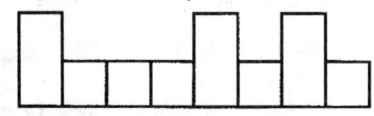

7. the B-29 which dropped the atomic bomb

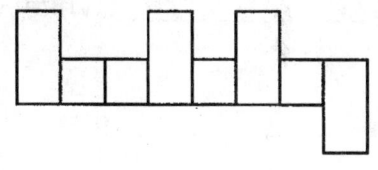

8. the descent of tiny particles of radioactive material

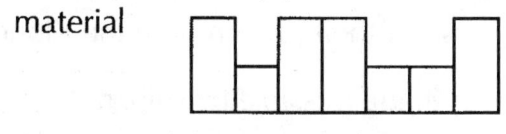

9. the ruins of the former Industrial Exhibition Hall

10. symptoms of this were vomiting, internal bleeding, hair loss, and fever

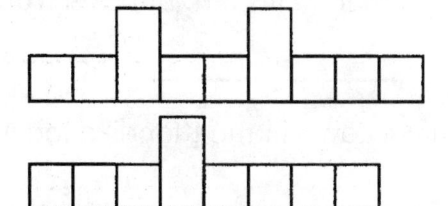

© Instructional Fair • TS Denison

IF8728 Challenge Your Mind

Panning in the Wild

name _____

Klondike Gold Discovery Day

Fill in the blanks with words from the Word Bank.

Word Bank

apart	enthusiast	million	news	removed	territory
book	gold	more	prospectors	rich	travel
Canada	magic	territory	rushed	Skagway	
crazy	many	mule	remains		

When gold was found at Rabbit Creek in the Yukon _____ of _____ in 1896, the _____ of its discovery spread quickly. By the following season folks were _____ with excitement. Adventurers from the world over _____ to the mining fields. One such _____ was Jack London who wrote about this _____ rush life in his _____ *White Fang*.

_____ than 30,000 people dashed for the gold. Many of these would-be _____ came by way of _____ or Valdez in Alaska because of their proximity to the Klondike region. _____ to the fields was made possible by ship, raft, _____, dogsled, and foot. _____, merchants, and thieves streamed in. Towns grew up like _____ in a very short time.

The gold strike fell _____ in 1910 and _____ of the prospectors and merchants left. But over 100 _____ dollars in ore had been _____. The town of Dawson, important then, _____ the major town in the Klondike today.

© Instructional Fair • TS Denison

IF8728 *Challenge Your Mind*

Well, Blow Me Down!

Name _____

America's Cup

On August 22, 1851, the first America's Cup was held. The U.S. became most interested in this "sport of the sea." In each set, can you change the first word into the last word by changing one letter at a time to match the definitions?

Set 1

SAIL	1st
_____	to send by post
_____	a shopping center with many stores
_____	opposite of a female
_____	an evil weapon
RACE	last

Set 2

WIND	1st
_____	a magician's rod
_____	to grow faint
WAVE	last

Set 3

SEA	1st
_____	a round green-pod veggie
_____	spunk
_____	a young seal
CUP	last

Set 4

MAST	1st
_____	like a chocolate shake
_____	to stop
_____	a corridor
HULL	last

Set 5

YAWL	1st
_____	to wail
_____	spherical toy
_____	to stop short
_____	behind
_____	to fire (slang)
_____	argyle
DOCK	last

THE U.S. HELD THE AMERICA'S CUP FROM 1851 TO 1980!

© Instructional Fair • TS Denison

IF8728 Challenge Your Mind

Being Equal

name _____

19th Amendment Day

Can you imagine a time when only men could vote? Until 1920, this was the practice in the United States. To read a quote from the 19th Amendment to the U.S. Constitution, fill in the blanks with letters from the chart in the order the code requires. Fill in letters from the first rows first, then move down until all letters are used. The first row has been started for you.

Code: 11-4-2-6-9-1-7-5-10-3-8

1	2	3	4	5	6	7	8	9	10	11
~~O~~	~~E~~	F	~~T~~	~~R~~	~~H~~	C	~~I~~	O	~~T~~
N	I	T	T	O	Z	S	H	E	F	I
E	N	A	U	S	I	D	T	T	T	E
O	T	H	S	E	O	T	A	V	S	E
B	N	N	L	D	O	E	I	T	E	L
B	O	G	D	I	R	R	E	A	D	E
E	Y	T	B	N	T	U	E	H	I	D
E	T	B	S	O	A	S	Y	T	R	D
A	Y	N	N	E	S	T	A	T	O	A
T	O	E	C	F	U	O	X	N	S	C

NEW ZEALAND GAVE WOMEN THE RIGHT TO VOTE IN 1893!

T H E   R I G H T __ __ __ __ __ __ __ __ __ __ __ __

__ __ __ __ __ __ __ __ __ __ __ __ __ __ __

__ __ __ __ __ __ __ __ __ __ __ __ __ __ __ __

__ __ __ __ __ __ __ __ __ __ __ __ __ __ __ __

__ __ __ __ __ __ __ __ __ __ __ __ __ __ __ .

Farewell, Summer!

Name _____

First Day of School

Bumbling Bob is ready for school with the purchase of twenty items. His list is a bit disorganized. Unscramble the words to figure out what he bought.

1. CEILNPS _____
2. AEENOPPRT _____
3. AEERRS _____
4. CEHLMNNOUY _____
5. EEFILNPPTT _____
6. AEHIRSSTTW _____
7. DEFLORS _____
8. EEHKOSSUY _____
9. CEGHLMOSTY _____
10. AACCLLORTU _____
11. AABCCKKP _____
12. AEKMRRS _____
13. CEGGHIMNUW _____
14. AEEJNNSW _____
15. BEKNOOOST _____
16. AACDFNOOS _____

© Instructional Fair • TS Denison

IF8728 Challenge Your Mind

Career Caper

name _____

Labor Day

On this day which honors workers in Canada and the United States, most people don't have to work! Is that strange, or what? Unscramble the words to list some of the possible occupations just waiting for you.

1. TTSIRA — A _ _ _ _ T
2. LTIIAIOPCN — P _ _ _ _ _ _ _ _ N
3. YTAOCRF RRWKOE — F _ _ _ _ _ _ _ _ _ _ _ R
4. CRRRSEEHEA — R _ _ _ _ _ _ _ _ R
5. RLECK — C _ _ _ K
6. SREETFRO — F _ _ _ _ _ _ R
7. TREIRW — W _ _ _ _ R
8. TRAUOCDE — E _ _ _ _ _ _ R
9. MARREF — F _ _ _ _ R
10. MEALSSAN — S _ _ _ _ _ _ N
11. NIECISTTS — S _ _ _ _ _ _ _ T
12. SEURN — N _ _ _ E
13. IENMR — M _ _ _ R
14. YNAIIHSPC — P _ _ _ _ _ _ _ N
15. TEALHET — A _ _ _ _ _ E
16. DBIRUEL — B _ _ _ _ _ R
17. NAIINCEHTC — T _ _ _ _ _ _ _ _ N
18. RATILO — T _ _ _ _ R
19. RANUITJOLS — J _ _ _ _ _ _ _ _ T
20. TTEEERRINNA — E _ _ _ _ _ _ _ _ _ _ R
21. LOCSAI RKOREW — S _ _ _ _ _ _ _ _ _ _ _ R

Speech bubble: MAYBE YOU COULD RAISE A HERD OF NAUGAS FOR LIKE, Y'KNOW... NAUGAHYDE!

© Instructional Fair • TS Denison

IF8728 Challenge Your Mind

Your Not-So-Distant Past

Name _____

Nat'l Grandparents Day

Fill in the blanks and identify the words below. Then use the clues from the completed words to complete the phrase at the bottom of the page.

1. given to reverie; visionary

   $\overline{22}\ \overline{39}\ \overline{3}\ \overline{40}\ \overline{34}\ \overline{9}$

2. six-sided polygons

   $\overline{2}\ \overline{28}\ \overline{6}\ \overline{35}\ \overline{38}\ \overline{44}\ \overline{18}\ \overline{25}$

3. an eating utensil

   $\overline{11}\ \overline{32}\ \overline{8}\ \overline{46}$

4. silly

   $\overline{43}\ \overline{30}\ \overline{14}\ \overline{45}\ \overline{17}\ \overline{23}\ \overline{27}$

5. spirit

   $\overline{48}\ \overline{13}\ \overline{5}\ \overline{36}\ \overline{20}$

6. coarse

   $\overline{19}\ \overline{8}\ \overline{15}\ \overline{26}\ \overline{1}\ \overline{31}$

7. fairly, rightfully

   $\overline{29}\ \overline{7}\ \overline{47}\ \overline{26}\ \overline{16}\ \overline{37}$

8. something carried; a burden

   $\overline{4}\ \overline{10}\ \overline{40}\ \overline{22}$

9. discoveries

   $\overline{33}\ \overline{21}\ \overline{18}\ \overline{42}\ \overline{24}\ \overline{41}\ \overline{19}\ \overline{12}$

Phrase:

$\overline{1}\ \overline{2}\ \overline{3}\ \ \overline{4}\ \overline{5}\ \overline{6}\ \overline{7}\ \overline{8}\ \overline{9}\ \ \overline{10}\ \overline{11}\ \ \overline{12}\ \overline{13}\ \overline{14}\ \overline{15}\ \overline{16}\ \overline{17}\ \overline{18}\ \overline{19}$

$\overline{20}\ \overline{21}\ \overline{22}\ \overline{23}\ \ \overline{24}\ \overline{25}\ \ \overline{26}\ \overline{27}\ \overline{28}\ \ \overline{29}\ \overline{30}\ \overline{31}\ \ \overline{32}\ \overline{33}\ \ \overline{34}\ \overline{35}\ \overline{36}\ \overline{37}$

$\overline{38}\ \overline{39}\ \overline{40}\ \overline{41}\ \overline{42}\ \overline{43}\ \overline{44}\ \overline{45}\ \overline{46}\ \overline{47}$

© Instructional Fair • TS Denison

IF8728 Challenge Your Mind

See You Real Soon

Name _____

Mickey Mouse's Birthday

It's the birthday of the most famous animated character of all time. Find 33 words related to Disney in the wordsearch including Mickey's names in French (Michel), Japanese (Miki), Spanish (Miguel), and Danish (Mikkel).

IS THIS PAGE A LITTLE GOOFY OR IS IT ME?

D	H	E	Y	E	N	S	I	D	E	W	E	Y	E	R
U	O	P	F	A	N	T	A	S	I	A	H	U	E	Y
M	M	N	L	I	C	E	B	E	G	O	O	R	C	S
B	I	E	A	A	L	A	A	L	S	M	Y	A	H	O
O	K	H	B	L	Y	M	M	E	M	O	N	T	R	U
G	K	L	C	S	D	B	B	H	I	U	I	O	I	R
O	E	C	I	U	M	O	I	C	G	S	M	N	S	I
O	L	A	I	N	K	A	N	I	U	E	I	O	T	S
F	D	R	M	O	R	T	I	M	E	R	J	C	M	I
Y	W	O	R	L	D	W	I	L	L	I	E	I	A	K
I	A	L	A	N	D	R	E	P	M	U	H	T	S	I
E	L	T	E	K	C	I	R	C	E	I	U	O	L	M
O	T	U	L	P	M	I	C	K	E	Y	K	C	U	D

Word Box

BAMBI	DISNEY	HUEY	MICHEL	MOUSE	SOURIS
CABLE	DONALD	JIMINY	MICKEY	MUS	STEAMBOAT
CAROL	DUCK	KUCHI	MIGUEL	PLAY	THUMPER
CHRISTMAS	DUMBO	LAND	MIKI	PLUTO	WALT
CRICKET	FANTASIA	LIFE	MIKKEL	RATONOCITO	WILLIE
DAISY	GOOFY	LOUIE	MORTIMER	SCROOGE	WORLD
DEWEY					

What do the eleven remaining letters spell? _____

© Instructional Fair • TS Denison

IF8728 *Challenge Your Mind*

Mr. Postman, Look and See

Write the words under the appropriate category.

Word Bank

selling stamps	delivering	letter	pouch	string
announcements	filing	mailbox	priority	tape
next-day-delivery	first class	postcards	airmail	C.O.D.
care package	gifts	certified	sorting	third class
greeting card	carrying	photos	stamping	uniform
parcel post	invitation	postage	stamps	weighing
transporting	envelope			

Jobs | **Tools of Mailing** | **What Is Sent** | **How Sent**

Here are some things you can do for the postal services:

1. Keep your pet restrained.
2. Write your address neatly on the envelope.
3. Keep a clear passage to your mailbox.
4. Say hello and smile at your carrier.
5. Send a thank you card to your service office.

YOU COULD REMEMBER TO PUT A STAMP ON THAT LETTER!

It's a (Cold) Snap!

name _____

First Day of Autumn

Choose partners from the word list related to fall to complete each crossword. You will not need all the words listed.

Word Partners

First Word		Second Word	
falling	color	parties	games
colder	world	geese	season
harvest	mixer	matches	bonfires
frosty	picking	leaves	flowers
football	raking	nights	yard
marching	drying	pumpkins	apples
caramel	making	series	temperatures
glorious	sweater	bands	time
soccer	honking	tours	colors

Grant Us Peace

Name _____

Provide a word from the Word Box to match each meaning. Then use clues from the completed answers to build a phrase honoring peace. Words in the phrase may wrap to a second line.

a. a partial payment $\overline{106}\ \overline{3}\ \overline{23}\ \overline{35}\ \overline{19}\ \overline{94}\ \overline{6}$

b. haughty $\overline{29}\ \overline{44}\ \overline{105}\ \overline{50}\ \overline{70}\ \overline{98}\ \overline{82}\ \overline{67}$

c. of subordinate importance $\overline{28}\ \overline{7}\ \overline{64}\ \overline{104}\ \overline{49}$

d. to cry $\overline{74}\ \overline{69}\ \overline{18}\ \overline{109}$

e. rebellions $\overline{53}\ \overline{21}\ \overline{81}\ \overline{88}\ \overline{93}$

f. a style of cooking $\overline{26}\ \overline{71}\ \overline{61}\ \overline{45}\ \overline{76}\ \overline{95}\ \overline{4}$

g. to fling $\overline{2}\ \overline{85}\ \overline{12}\ \overline{37}$

h. an injury $\overline{34}\ \overline{84}\ \overline{51}\ \overline{72}\ \overline{42}$

i. fit and hale $\overline{46}\ \overline{66}\ \overline{100}\ \overline{55}\ \overline{92}\ \overline{75}\ \overline{30}$

j. to disable $\overline{15}\ \overline{36}\ \overline{111}\ \overline{79}\ \overline{99}\ \overline{62}\ \overline{47}$

k. very dirty $\overline{20}\ \overline{89}\ \overline{13}\ \overline{1}\ \overline{68}\ \overline{103}$

l. to comprehend $\overline{32}\ \overline{58}\ \overline{14}\ \overline{107}\ \overline{90}\ \overline{60}\ \overline{101}\ \overline{54}\ \overline{5}\ \overline{38}$

m. weariless $\overline{96}\ \overline{17}\ \overline{112}\ \overline{40}\ \overline{56}\ \overline{9}\ \overline{73}\ \overline{87}$

n. a first-class aviator $\overline{110}\ \overline{77}\ \overline{63}$

o. an entrance $\overline{38}\ \overline{31}\ \overline{97}\ \overline{8}$

p. to listen $\overline{102}\ \overline{24}\ \overline{48}\ \overline{33}$

q. a strap for walking a dog $\overline{39}\ \overline{43}\ \overline{25}\ \overline{108}\ \overline{78}$

r. a paddle $\overline{11}\ \overline{57}\ \overline{22}$

s. anxious $\overline{10}\ \overline{80}\ \overline{52}\ \overline{86}\ \overline{91}\ \overline{27}\ \overline{83}$

t. game item $\overline{65}\ \overline{41}\ \overline{16}\ \overline{59}$

Word Box

understand	cuisine	hear	filthy	healthy	cripple	coups
ace	weep	leash	oar	minor	tireless	door
worried	wound	deposit	hurl	arrogant	card	

Grapple with Apples

name _____

Johnny Appleseed's Birthday

What a wonderful day to think about apples! For each set, change the first word into the last *apple-inspired* word by changing one letter at a time to match the definitions.

Set 1

fan	1st word
_____	baking platter
_____	sharp fastener
_____	tasty dessert

Set 2

bolts	1st word
_____	these hold up pants
_____	chimes
_____	tummy
_____	bread spread

Set 3

chap	1st word
_____	a crunchy potato
_____	under the mouth
_____	lean
_____	one's clone
_____	from which an apple hangs

Set 4

place	1st word
_____	shallow dish
_____	type of rock
_____	a sudden flood
_____	malice
_____	to inflict a blow
_____	Granny's apple

Set 5

pit	1st word
_____	set on fire
_____	cover
_____	boy
_____	his pa
_____	opposite of night
_____	speak
_____	a sneaky apple variety

WOULD AN APPLE A DAY KEEP THIS PROBLEM AWAY?

© Instructional Fair • TS Denison

IF8728 *Challenge Your Mind*

A Season to Praise

name _____

Sukkoth

During the festival of Sukkoth, sometimes called the Feast of Tabernacles, the people build shelters called *sukkah,* which are covered with greens and decorated with harvest foods. Traditionally the holiday is a memorial to the time the Israelites wandered in the desert after they left Egypt. Each word defined below will fit alphabetically between the two words shown. The number of letters matches the blanks provided.

SUKKOTH IS ONE OF THE THREE JOYOUS PILGRIM FESTIVALS OF JUDAISM!

1. bugle   _ _ _ _ _   bulb   to construct

2. Custer   _ _ _ _ _   cut   a tradition

3. bottom   _ _ _ _   boulder   a branch or limb

4. hart   _ _ _ _ _ _   has-been   to gather the crop

5. booted   _ _ _ _ _   bootleg   a covered or enclosed stand

6. automatic   _ _ _ _ _ _   auxiliary   season before winter

7. willing   _ _ _ _ _ _   willpower   the weeping tree

8. reject   _ _ _ _ _ _ _   rejoin   to express gladness

9. remedial   _ _ _ _ _   remiss   to prod into remembering

10. pallor   _ _ _ _   palooka   the tropical tree with dates

© Instructional Fair • TS Denison

IF8728 *Challenge Your Mind*

A Hot Time in the Old Town Tonight

name _____

Fire Prevention Week

Firefighters of North America are among the best in the world. Their work in our communities is vital to the safety of all. Take time to thank them this week.

Match the words from List #2 to their antonymns in List #1. Write the appropriate letters on the lines in front of each number. Not all words from list 2 will be used. Remember that antonyms are words that mean the opposite.

List 1

____ 1. alarming
____ 2. emergency
____ 3. help
____ 4. protected
____ 5. rescue
____ 6. adverse
____ 7. friend
____ 8. respond
____ 9. safety
____ 10. order
____ 11. healthy
____ 12. rush
____ 13. heat
____ 14. clean
____ 16. vigorous

List 2

a. chill
b. unguarded
c. dirty
d. ordinariness
e. plan
f. ignore
g. ailing
h. lethargic
i. crew
j. meander

k. favorable
l. recklessness
m. calm
n. chaos
o. endanger
p. hinder
q. soothing
r. opponent
s. radio

AWW... SHUCKS!

© Instructional Fair • TS Denison

IF8728 *Challenge Your Mind*

Charting the Explorers

name _____

Columbus Day

Fill in this chart using words that begin with the letters shown at the top of each column. Find as many as you can. You may use information sources to help you search. Have 2 or 3 others complete charts too. Then compare your answers, crossing out any duplicates. See which person has the most squares marked.

	S	H	I	P	S
Transportation					
Native American Tribes/Families					
Verbs Related to Exploration					
Languages of the World					
Occupations from the 15–16th Centuries					

© Instructional Fair • TS Denison

IF8728 Challenge Your Mind

Explor-a-tion

Name _____

Columbus Day

Add letter groups to each of these *-tion* endings to find words which fit the phrases below.

Letter Groups

an	da	fas	hi	la	na	per	pre	ra	sti	ta	ti	vi
ci	ex	frus	in	mi	pa	plo	ra	sen	su	ter	tra	vi
ci	ex	ga	in	na	pa	pre	ra	si	ta	ti	ven	

1. In order to get funding for his voyage, Columbus had to make a _____   _ _ _ _ _ _ _ _ t i o n

2. Columbus' hope for reaching the Far East filled him with _____   _ _ _ _ _ _ _ _ t i o n

3. Upon reaching land, Columbus might very well have experienced overwhelming _____   _ _ _ _ _ _ _ _ t i o n

4. When Columbus reached the New World, he spent much time in _____   _ _ _ _ _ _ _ t i o n

5. When his officers quarreled, Columbus may have been required to use _____   _ _ _ _ _ _ _ _ t i o n

6. To sail the seas, Columbus had to possess skills of _____   _ _ _ _ _ t i o n

7. Columbus' love of maps bordered on this _____   _ _ _ _ _ _ t i o n

8. Organizing for the voyages undoubtedly meant much _____   _ _ _ _ _ _ _ t i o n

9. The native people may have hoped the Europeans' first _____ would be their last   _ _ _ _ _ _ t i o n

10. When they could not easily persuade native people to help them, the Europeans sometimes resorted to _____   _ _ _ _ _ _ _ t i o n

11. Because Columbus never reached China, he may have experienced _____   _ _ _ _ _ t i o n

12. _____ led some explorers to fear sea monsters and singing sea maids   _ _ _ _ _ _ _ t i o n

© Instructional Fair • TS Denison

IF8728 *Challenge Your Mind*

Papa Wordsmith

On October 16, 1758, Mr. Noah Webster was born. We remember him for his labor with an American-English Dictionary. Decode the symbols below to find these Webster-minded words.

A	B	C	D	E	F	G	H	I	J	K	L	M	N	O	P	Q	R	S	T	U	V	W	X	Y	Z
+	=	:	;	"	'	?	/	,	.	[	]	|	\	!	@	#	$	%	^	&	*	(	)	<	>

1. ALLITERATION
2. FORESHADOW
3. LINGUISTICS
4. SYNTAX
5. VERBOSE
6. DIALECT
7. ETYMOLOGY
8. OXYMORON
9. EUPHEMISM
10. TERMINOLOGY
11. PUN
12. ACCENT
13. ORATORY
14. LEXICOGRAPHIC

Locate five of these words in the dictionary and write their meanings on the back of this sheet.

We Are the World

name _____

United Nations Day

This august council of world representatives, the United Nations, is more than fifty years old. Unscramble the puzzled words to learn more.

1. The United Nations was established in (NETINENE YRTFO EFIV) _____ .

2. The U.N. began with (IFYTF - NEO) _____ -member countries.

3. Three main goals of the U.N. are to:

   a. maintain international (ACEEP) _____ ,

   b. promote (AELQU ITGRHS) _____ _____ ,

   c. and achieve (ACEEIOOPRTV) _____ solutions to world problems.

4. The six main bodies of the U.N. are:

   a. the General (ABELMSSY) _____ ,

   b. the (CEIRSTUY LOINUCC) _____ _____ ,

   c. the (CCEIMNOO) _____ and Social Council,

   d. the (EEHIPRSSTTU) _____ Council,

   e. the (AACEEIRRSTT) _____ ,

   f. and the International (CORTU) _____ of Justice.

5. The Security Council has 15 representative countries of which five are permanent members. These five are:

   a. (ACHIN) _____   d. (DEINTU AESSTT) _____

   b. (ACEFNR) _____   e. (DEINTU DIGKMNO) _____

   c. (AIRSSU) _____

6. The six official languages of the U.N. are:

   a. (AABCIR) _____   d. (CERHNF) _____

   b. (CEEHINS) _____   e. (AINRSSU) _____

   c. (EGHILNS) _____   f. (AHINPSS) _____

© Instructional Fair • TS Denison

IF8728 Challenge Your Mind

Know Your World

name _____

United Nations Day

Unscramble the names of twenty countries of our world. Some are near and some are distant. The continent where each country can be found has been given as a clue.

Country   **Continents**

1. ADEILNRSTWZ _____ Europe
2. YENKA _____ Africa
3. AEEGLNS _____ Africa
4. AGRUUUY _____ South America
5. ABINOS _____ Europe
6. OLVBIAI _____ South America
7. AIRSY _____ Asia
8. CCMOOOR _____ Africa
9. LAZRIB _____ South America
10. AAAACDGMRS _____ Africa
11. ADEIINNOS _____ Asia
12. AABCDIMO _____ Asia
13. AGLOPRTU _____ Europe
14. ACDEILN _____ Europe
15. AAACDN _____ North America
16. BEGILMU _____ Europe
17. AEINOST _____ Europe
18. AAGNUY _____ South America

Things That Go Bump

name _____

Halloween

Complete this word fill-in with the words supplied.

3 Letters—bag boo gum

4 Letters—dark howl wigs wind

5 Letters—apple black broom candy ghoul gourd masks scary sheet treat witch

6 Letters—dreary ghosts make-up orange scream spooky sweets zombie

7 Letters—candles costume evening goblins haunted mansion pumpkin spiders vampire

8 Letters—black cat monsters tricking

9 Letters—bed sheets cornstalk doorbells lightning scarecrow

10 Letters—an owl's hoot face paints flashlight pillowcase

11 Letters—fluorescent Devil's Night

12 Letters—jack-'o-lantern

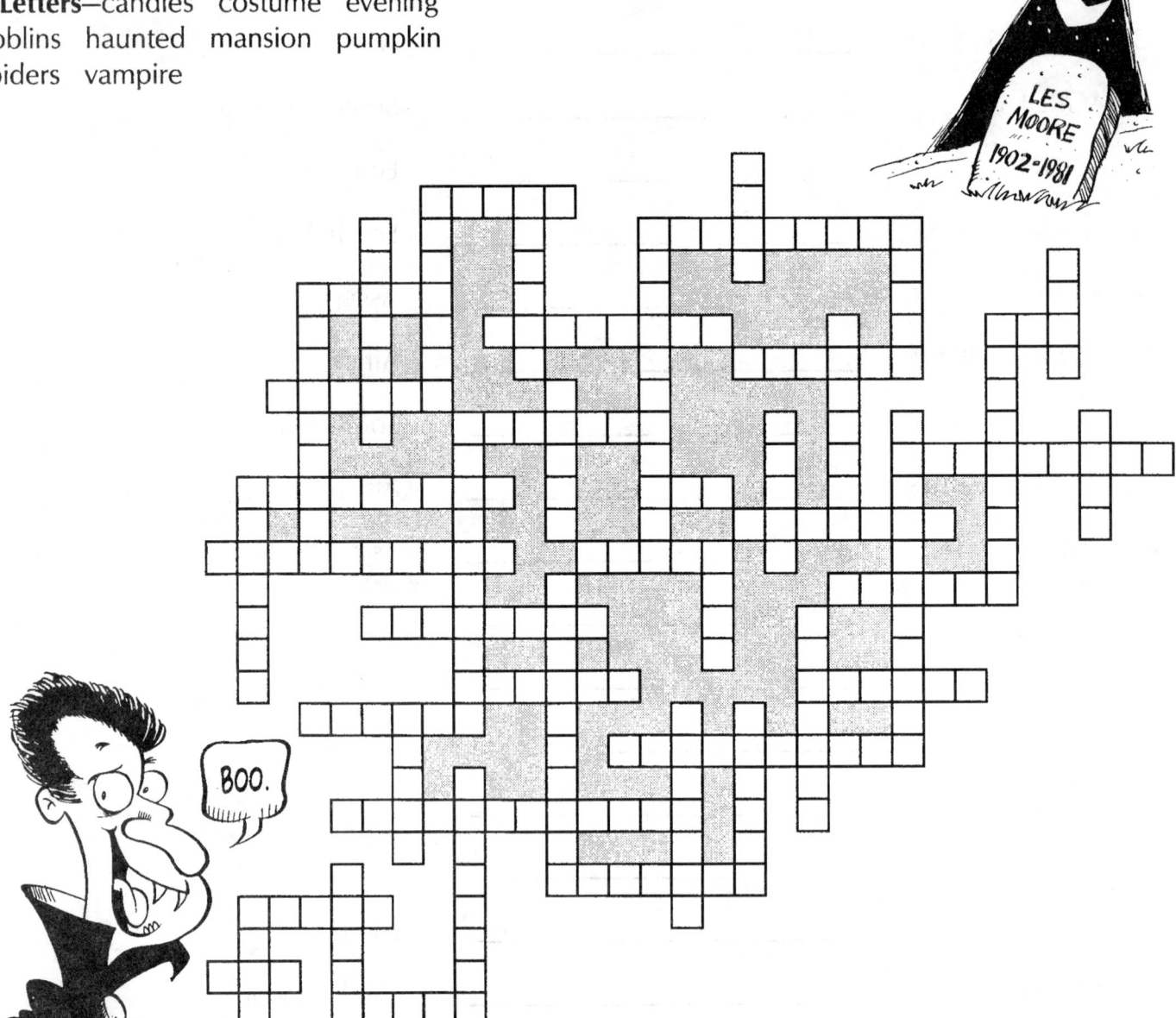

© Instructional Fair • TS Denison

IF8728 Challenge Your Mind

A Frightful Custom

Name _____

Fit the Word Box words sensibly into the sentences.

Word Box
carrying
prosperous
spirits
festival
year
devil
performing
popular
escape
ghosts
community
lights
evil
willingly
returned
countries
outdoors
costumes

The Celtic _____ of Samhain marked the last day of the Celtic _____ . These early Celts believed that the _____ of the dead _____ on this evening. Food and _____ were placed outside houses so these _____ would feel at home.

In later times, people who went _____ after dark would wear _____ so witches and other evil spirts would not recognize them. In some villages, the townsfolk would go house to house begging for food for their _____ feasts. Those who _____ and big-heartedly gave food would be guaranteed a _____ new year.

According to Irish legend, a most _____ man named Jack tricked the devil. Because he was not fit for heaven and because the _____ would not accept him, this Jack, upon death, was forced to walk about Earth _____ a gourd, a *jack-o'-lantern*.

Halloween became _____ in the U.S. and Canada as Irish families immigrated into these _____ in the 1800s.

Harry Houdini, the eminent _____ artist, died while _____ on this day in 1926.

© Instructional Fair • TS Denison

IF8728 *Challenge Your Mind*

Hindu Festival of Lights

Name _____

Diwali

LAKSHMI IS ALSO THE WIFE OF HINDU GOD VISHNU!

Diwali is the holiday of India that signifies the end of harvest and the beginning of winter. During this festival **Lakshmi**, the Hindu goddess of good luck and prosperity, comes to people's homes and is greeted by lamps called *dipa*.

Fit the letters in each column into the boxes directly above them to form words. The letters may or may not go into the boxes in the same order in which they are given. Some words may wrap to the next line. Your finished puzzle is a plea to this goddess.

| C | O | M | E | | | | | | | | | | | | | | | | | | | | | | |

(puzzle grid with letters below:)

Row: C E H C A I A R E E O H E O G O D D E E A E N C E M A A
Row: L O M O A I D T F O R U I S H O M E R H O K O F I W E O
Row: R T Y W U N N O T W R H R T O L S N O H Y F U
Row: W T W Y U P S S S R O

Word Box

Goddess	wealth	are	your	into	presence
you (2)	honor	wait	wish	honor	the
home	Lakshima	and	of	our	to
come	for (2)	we (2)			

© Instructional Fair • TS Denison

82

IF8728 Challenge Your Mind

Add or Subtract

name _____

All Saints' Day

When the early Christian church set aside a day to honor the many saints killed for their faith, they chose the day of Samhain, a feared day which recalled spirits of the dead and evil beings. In this activity, add to, or subtract letters from the words listed to form a word or phrase associated with these two holidays.

Letter Bank A C E E F I M M O R R T T U X̶

1. stolen key   -y   _skeleton_   structural body organ
2. sane trap   ___   _____   serf
3. frame   ___   _____   dread
4. cards   ___   _____   holy
5. pang   ___   _____   heathen
6. rustiest point   ___   _____   belief in omens
7. trial   ___   _____   rite
8. mend   ___   _____   devil
9. thread   ___   _____   demise
10. meal   ___   _____   fire
11. whit   ___   _____   sorceress
12. sat gave   ___   _____   wild
13. tarry   ___   _____   life sacrificer
14. trips   ___   _____   ghost

© Instructional Fair • TS Denison   IF8728 *Challenge Your Mind*

Writer's Niche

name _____

Author's Day

Fill in this chart using words that begin with the letters shown at the side of each column. The columns are independent of one another. In other words, you don't have to list a work written by the author you list. Find as many as you can. You may use information sources to help your search. Have 2 or 3 others complete charts too. Then compare your answers, crossing out any duplicates. See which person has the most squares unmarked.

	Last Names of Famous Authors	Writers' Tools	Types of Writing	Writers' Actions	Works of Famous Fiction
W					
R					
I					
T					
E					
R					

© Instructional Fair • TS Denison

IF8728 Challenge Your Mind

I'll Have a Dagwood, Please

Name _____

National Sandwich Day

Using the Word Box, write synonyms for the bold-faced words in the blanks.

We think sandwiches were **invented** _____ by John Montagu, the Fourth Earl of Sandwich, who was so **attracted** _____ to gambling that he refused to leave his card table to grab a **bite** _____ . The **account** _____ declares that he **dispatched** _____ his servant to obtain some meat to **place** _____ between two slices of bread. When the other **patrons** _____ saw the order which the returning servant **carried** _____ , they did not forget. Sandwiches have been with us ever since.

Sandwiches are as **varied** _____ as humans. Sandwiches may be **made** _____ from bagels, croissants, and pita bread. They may be **little** _____ triangles or six-foot-long crowd-**suited** _____ inventions. They may **hold** _____ peanut butter or roast beef. They may consist of **fresh** _____ vegetables and mayonnaise. Or they may be **filled** _____ with **hot dogs** _____ and sauerkraut.

Did you **know** _____ the Sandwich Islands were **named** _____ to honor this 18th century lord? Now we call these islands *Hawaii*, but when Captain James Cook **arrived at** _____ them in 1778, he named them after his **boss** _____ , John Montagu.

Word Box

accommodate	clients	diverse	loaded	narrative	realize	stick
assembled	devised	dubbed	lured	petite	sent	uncooked
bore	director	frankfurters	meal	reached	serving	

© Instructional Fair • TS Denison

IF8728 *Challenge Your Mind*

Bring on the New!

name _____

Election Day

Ann, Fran, Jan, and Nan can usually agree on the important things in their lives. Yet, when the political elections came up today, they found that they were miles apart in their thinking. Match each girl to her candidate of choice (first and last name) and decide which single issue was most important to each voter.

1. Fran, for whom either foreign affairs or finance is a burning issue, voted for neither Dobb nor Noah.
2. Ann and Jan favored male candidates, neither of whom made finance their primary issue.
3. The four voters are the one who supports Sobb, the one whose key issue is crime, Nan, and the one choosing Louis.
4. Megan's last name is either Robb or Sobb. She is a finance wizard.
5. Ann does not vote for Sobb. The one who votes for Louis is not interested in women's issues. Jan has an interest in foreign affairs.
6. Mr. Robb is strong on neither foreign affairs nor the issues of women.
7. Louis is either Nobb or Sobb.

	Dobb	Nobb	Robb	Sobb	Foreign Affairs	Finance	Women	Crime	Louis	Megan	Noah	Sandra
Ann												
Fran												
Jan												
Nan												
Louis												
Megan												
Noah												
Sandra												
for. aff.												
finance												
women												
crime												

IT'S THE AMERICAN WAY!

© Instructional Fair • TS Denison

IF8728 Challenge Your Mind

Crazy Cryptics

name _____

Election Day

All the words in this cryptic puzzle follow the same code. A set of letters has been substituted for the correct letter in each word. All of these words have something to do with the election process. Can you figure them out?

Clues:
1. The letter H represents E.
2. The letter E represents S.
3. The letter L represents O.
4. The letter I represents P.

1. ZLYBTA _____
2. ALZHOTLO _____
3. VHRLJOKYE _____
4. JKRIKBAT _____
5. HBAMYHHT _____
6. JLTAOHEE _____
7. OHIQUGBJKTE _____
8. RKSLO _____
9. ULLYM _____
10. IOLRBEHE _____
11. IOLILEKGE _____
12. EHTKYLO _____
13. UKGGLY _____
14. YZKVE _____
15. IOHEBVHTY _____

THE RIGHT TO VOTE IS, LIKE, THE CORNERSTONE OF DEMOCRACY!

© Instructional Fair • TS Denison

IF8728 Challenge Your Mind

Over There!

name _____

Veterans Day

November 11 marks the end of World War I or *the Great War* as it was called then. Some people call this day *Armistice Day*. This war involved the use of trenches, mustard gas, machine guns, and tank warfare for the first time.

Match the words in the left column to the synonyms on the right. Place the appropriate letter in front of each number. Not all words in the second column will be used.

____ 1. horse soldiers
____ 2. conquest
____ 3. doughboy
____ 4. armored vehicle
____ 5. cooties
____ 6. captive
____ 7. victim
____ 8. camouflage
____ 9. arms
____ 10. ruination
____ 11. armistice
____ 12. attack
____ 13. crowds
____ 14. ally
____ 15. frontier
____ 16. war
____ 17. trenches
____ 18. army meal

a. truce
b. rations
c. partner
d. cavalry
e. border
f. victory
g. offensive
h. masses
i. conflict
j. ditches
k. prisoner
l. surrender
m. disguise
n. uniform
o. tank
p. weapons
q. lice
r. casualty
s. destruction
t. soldier
u. battle

ARMISTICE DAY WAS CHANGED TO VETERANS DAY IN 1954!

© Instructional Fair • TS Denison

IF8728 *Challenge Your Mind*

A Picture's Worth ...

name _____

Thanksgiving

Match the words with the appropriate picture. As you write down the name of each picture in the correct spot, the words reading vertically in the bold line will spell a Thanksgiving Day message. Two of the pictures will be used twice.

1. 3-masted
2. finger
3. black
4. snow
5. bird
6. pilgrim
7. Macy's
8. football
9. fried
10. bear
11. drum
12. olive
13. Indian
14. scrumptious
15. corn
16. turkey
17. grandmother's
18. rose
19. pumpkin
20. Plymouth

© Instructional Fair • TS Denison

IF8728 Challenge Your Mind

A Thanksgiving Puzzle

name _____

Thanksgiving

Find the six-letter words defined below. Then trace them in order in the puzzle beginning with the boxed square. In this puzzle the last letter of a word becomes the first letter of the next word. You will use all the letters.

Definition   **Word**

1. the Thanksgiving bird _____
2. color of sweet corn kernel _____
3. how a duck or goose might walk _____
4. the use of energy to do something _____
5. the serving dishes are placed on these _____
6. holy _____
7. trenchers, bowls, platters _____
8. companionable, gregarious _____
9. mourn or grieve for _____
10. to journey _____
11. timber cut for building use _____
12. misgiving _____
13. gratitude _____
14. freedom from danger _____

THE FIRST NATIONAL THANKSGIVING DAY WAS CELEBRATED NOVEMBER 26, 1789!

E	K	R	I	S	H	E	S
Y	E	U	D	E	R	C	O
L	L	T	R	T	C	I	A
O	D	D	O	A	A	A	L
W	A	L	F	B	S	M	E
B	M	E	F	L	E	T	N
E	U	L	E	V	A	R	★
R	R	E	A	N	Y	T	E
E	G	T	H	K	S	A	F

© Instructional Fair • TS Denison

IF8728 *Challenge Your Mind*

Turkey Time

name _____

Thanksgiving

Write the words which match the descriptions below. Need clues? Unscramble the words at the bottom of the page to help discover the answers.

1. _____ 1. children + parents = _____

2. _____ 2. festive drink for the holidays

3. _____ 3. emotion of great affection

4. _____ 4. mirth + giggles = _____

5. _____ 5. the first; the beginning

6. _____ 6. opposite of coldness

7. _____ 7. food put into turkey's cavity before roasting

8. _____ 8. pig's meat

9. _____ 9. a request to come and celebrate

10. _____ 10. early American thankful folk

ABE LINCOLN MADE THANKSGIVING A NATIONAL HOLIDAY IN 1863!

Clues

amh	ggegon	iiiaonnttv
levo	fnuisfgt	garuhlet
iiaglnro	lafyim	hatmwr
rsigipml		

Now, use the first letter of each answer to find a word associated with this holiday.

___ ___ ___ ___ ___ ___ ___ ___ ___

© Instructional Fair • TS Denison

IF8728 Challenge Your Mind

Festival of Lights

name _____

The Jewish celebration of Hanukkah reminds Jewish people around the world of an important event in their history—a miracle that happened in their struggle against a powerful enemy.

Match each word from the Word Box to its definition. The letter boxes may help you do this more easily.

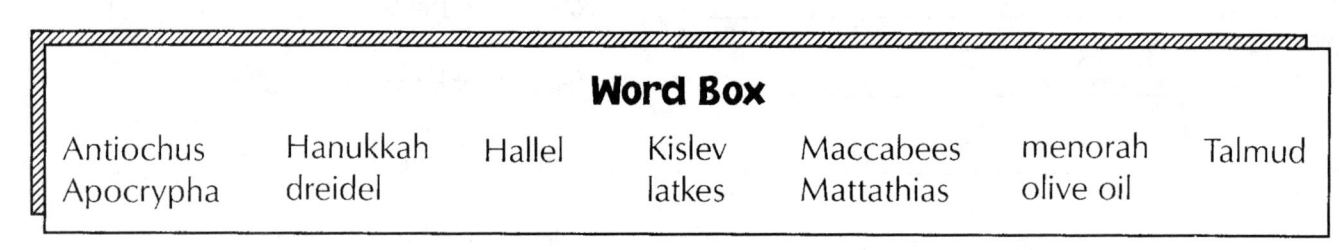

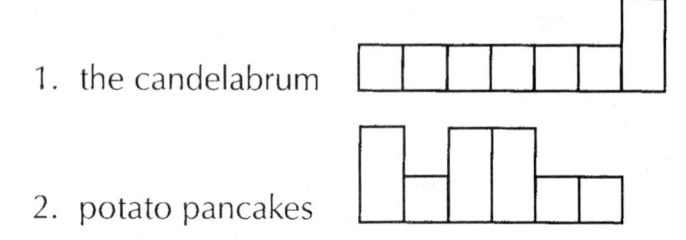

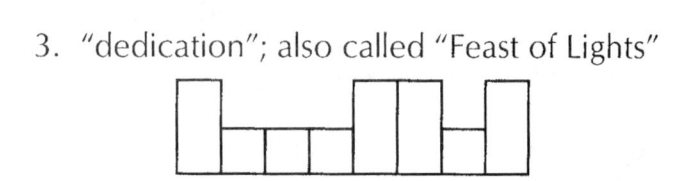

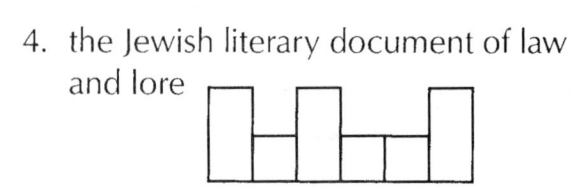

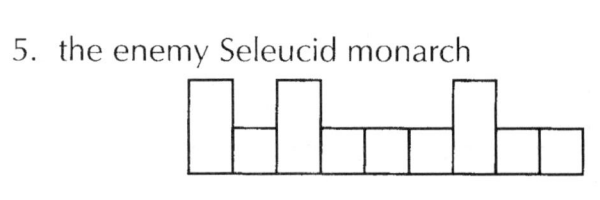

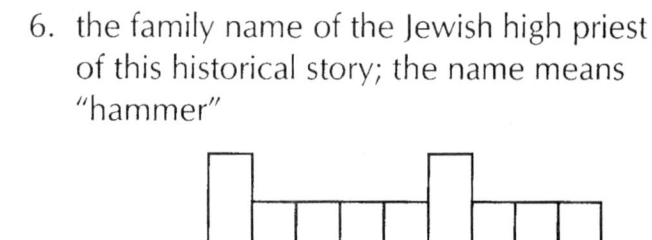

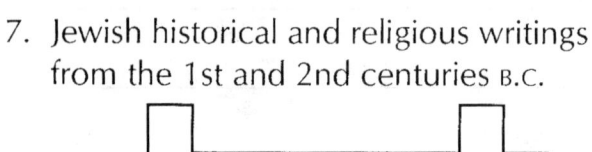

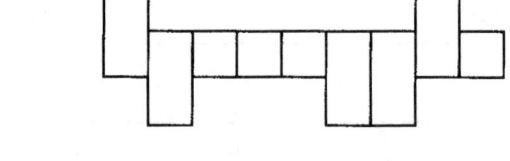

Word Box

| Antiochus | Hanukkah | Hallel | Kislev | Maccabees | menorah | Talmud |
| Apocrypha | dreidel | | latkes | Mattathias | olive oil | |

1. the candelabrum
2. potato pancakes
3. "dedication"; also called "Feast of Lights"
4. the Jewish literary document of law and lore
5. the enemy Seleucid monarch
6. the family name of the Jewish high priest of this historical story; the name means "hammer"
7. Jewish historical and religious writings from the 1st and 2nd centuries B.C.
8. the old Jewish priest who began this historical revolt
9. the Jewish month in which Hanukkah is celebrated
10. a 4-sided top used in this celebrative time
11. fuel used for the menorah
12. praise psalms

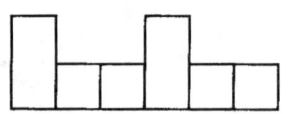

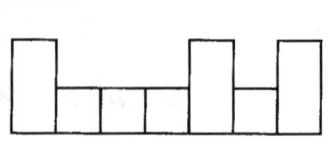

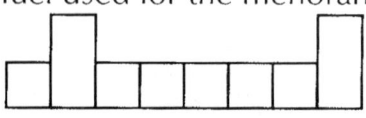

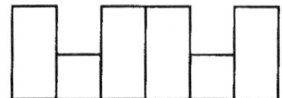

© Instructional Fair • TS Denison

IF8728 Challenge Your Mind

A Right Jolly Fellow

St. Nicholas Day

name _____

The legends of Saint Nicholas are old and varied. Many countries claim ownership of this Christian saint. Insert the 21 letters from the Letter Bank into the empty boxes to form words related to the saint's stories. The letter you insert may be the first, the last, or in the middle of the word. Cross out letters in the Letter Bank as you use them. The numbers along the side give the length for that line's word. Your finished list from top to bottom will give two foreign names for this saint.

Letter Bank: A A E E E E I K L L N N O O P R R R S S T

P	N	W	I					4
K	S	L	E					6
O	R	E	I					8
A	S	W	I					8
T	M	M	L					5
E	B	E	A					5
C	H	U	C					8
W	Z	B	E					5
J	T	O	C					5
P	A	D	S					5
U	R	E	D					7
I	O	Q	T					5
F	B	N	O					5
N	Z	S	E					4
C	G	I	V					5
T	M	E	R					5
Y	U	C	B					5
C	H	I	M					7
H	S	P	H					5
S	O	L	D					5
Y	D	W	A					7

E	J	X	O				
G	H	A	I				
D	E	E	R				
C	H	E	S				
L	V	E	S				
D	L	H	K				
L	E	S	E				
L	S	U	D				
N	D	Y	L				
I	N	T	F				
U	I	T	N				
U	C	H	G				
T	H	R	V				
O	L	E	A				
R	V	B	A				
Y	W	U	R				
L	L	Y	Q				
E	Y	I	G				
R	S	E	E				
N	F	X	M				
K	I	N	G				

SAINT NICHOLAS IS THE PATRON SAINT OF RUSSIA, CHILDREN AND SAILORS!

© Instructional Fair • TS Denison

IF8728 Challenge Your Mind

Fly Away Home

name _____

Wright Brothers First Flight

Match the words and phrases in the Word Box with the correct category headings.

Word Box

aileron	DC-3	frame	jacket	propeller	sunglasses	ultralight
biplane	dip	fuselage	jet	rise	supersonic	uniform
cable	dive	glide	lift	roll	airliner	visor
B-52	elevator	glider	nose	rudder	swoop	wings
climb	engine	goggles	pedal	seaplane		
controls	flaps	headphone	plunge	shuttle		
cruise	flight suit	helmet	pitch	soar		

Aviator Wear   **Flight Actions**   **Plane Parts**   **Plane Types**

CHARLES LINDBERGH WAS THE FIRST TO FLY SOLO ACROSS THE ATLANTIC OCEAN!

IT TOOK 33-1/2 HOURS!

© Instructional Fair • TS Denison

IF8728 *Challenge Your Mind*

Northern Climes

When winter arrives in the northern latitudes, people know they must adjust to the season change. Complete this crossword puzzle about this chilly time.

Across

3. long foot gear for traversing snowy terrain
5. a precipitant mixture of rain and snow
7. the neck wrap for a cold day
9. a steamy beverage made from the cacao seed
10. frozen rinks of ice are good for this
15. a long, flat-bottomed wooden sled
17. symptoms of this are coughing and sneezing
19. the supposed sleigh-pullers on December 24
20. snow wall from behind which snowball-laden warriors sally forth
21. a pile of snow shaped by wind
23. the foreclosure of academic studies (sometimes associated with 7 down)

Down

1. celestial images made while lying prone in the snow
2. chubby snow statues, like Frosty
4. melted and refrozen snow formation which hangs from roofs
5. the tubby senior elf of northern lore
6. dump _____ are used by some cities to haul away excess snow
7. a blizzard
8. this occurs when the dew point is below 0 degrees Celsius
11. large vehicles used to scrape snow from roadways
12. the solstice reached in late December
13. warm handwear utilized particularly by the young
14. a traveling condition considered a driver's nightmare
16. the seemingly lower temperature due to excessive breeze
18. long underwear
22. fuel for the fireplace

Ho Ho ... Oh No!

Name _____

Christmas

Find the 35 Christmas words hidden in the wordsearch below.

DO YOU KNOW WHAT BOXING DAY IS?

E	E	L	G	N	I	M	A	E	R	D	E	B	F
E	D	I	U	G	F	I	G	G	Y	L	H	T	O
T	O	O	B	E	L	L	S	H	F	L	O	S	G
N	O	S	E	O	A	P	P	A	R	E	L	A	G
E	R	W	S	R	U	D	O	L	F	M	L	O	Y
T	E	E	N	D	C	G	D	E	C	K	Y	T	J
S	E	T	D	E	T	I	H	W	V	O	Y	I	E
I	D	I	H	G	I	E	L	S	J	E	A	D	H
L	N	H	V	S	G	N	I	D	I	T	N	I	G
G	I	W	O	N	S	T	A	R	N	W	G	N	U
A	E	F	L	I	A	S	S	A	W	L	E	G	A
B	R	I	G	H	T	S	S	E	L	B	L	S	L

Word List

ale	boot	elf	glisten	laugh	Santa	tidings (2)	white (2)
angel	boughs	eve	guide	nose	sleigh	toast	wish
apparel	bright	figgy	holly	pudding	snow	town	
bells	deck	foggy	jolly	reindeer	star	wassail	
bless	dreaming	glee	joy	Rudolf			

Use six to eight of the words to write a sentence about Christmas.

_____

_____

Sing Lullaby

name _____

Christmas

Match the words from the Word Box with their synonyms. Write the words in the boxes provided.

Word Box

baby	musical
candy	peace
carol	present
cold	ring
jolly	rosy
joy	sleigh
light	sparkle
love	

HUH..?

tuneful / ariose / melodic	gift / boon / largesse	ruddy / flushed / glowing
shimmer / glitter / scintillation	jocund / mirthful / festive	sled / carriage / sledge	confection / sweets / treat
infant / neonate / bambino	chant / tune / vocalize	cheer / bliss / happiness	devotion / fancy / adoration
illumination / incandescence / luminosity	chime / knell / peal	nippy / boreal / arctic	calm / repose / tranquility

© Instructional Fair • TS Denison

IF8728 Challenge Your Mind

Sing We Merrily

name _____

Christmas is a time of singing. Here are song phrases both religious and secular. Choose word phrases from the list below as you complete each crossword. Be careful! You will not use all phrases on the list.

Phrase List

boughs of holly	gloria in excelsis Deo	peace and goodwill
bells on bobtail	merry little Christmas	what child is this
silent night	'tis the season	Christmas time in the city
oh Christmas tree	hark! the herald angels	sleigh ride together
good King Wenceslaus	sweetly singing	your Christmases be white
away in a manger	one-horse open sleigh	
figgy pudding	Rudolf the red-nosed reindeer	

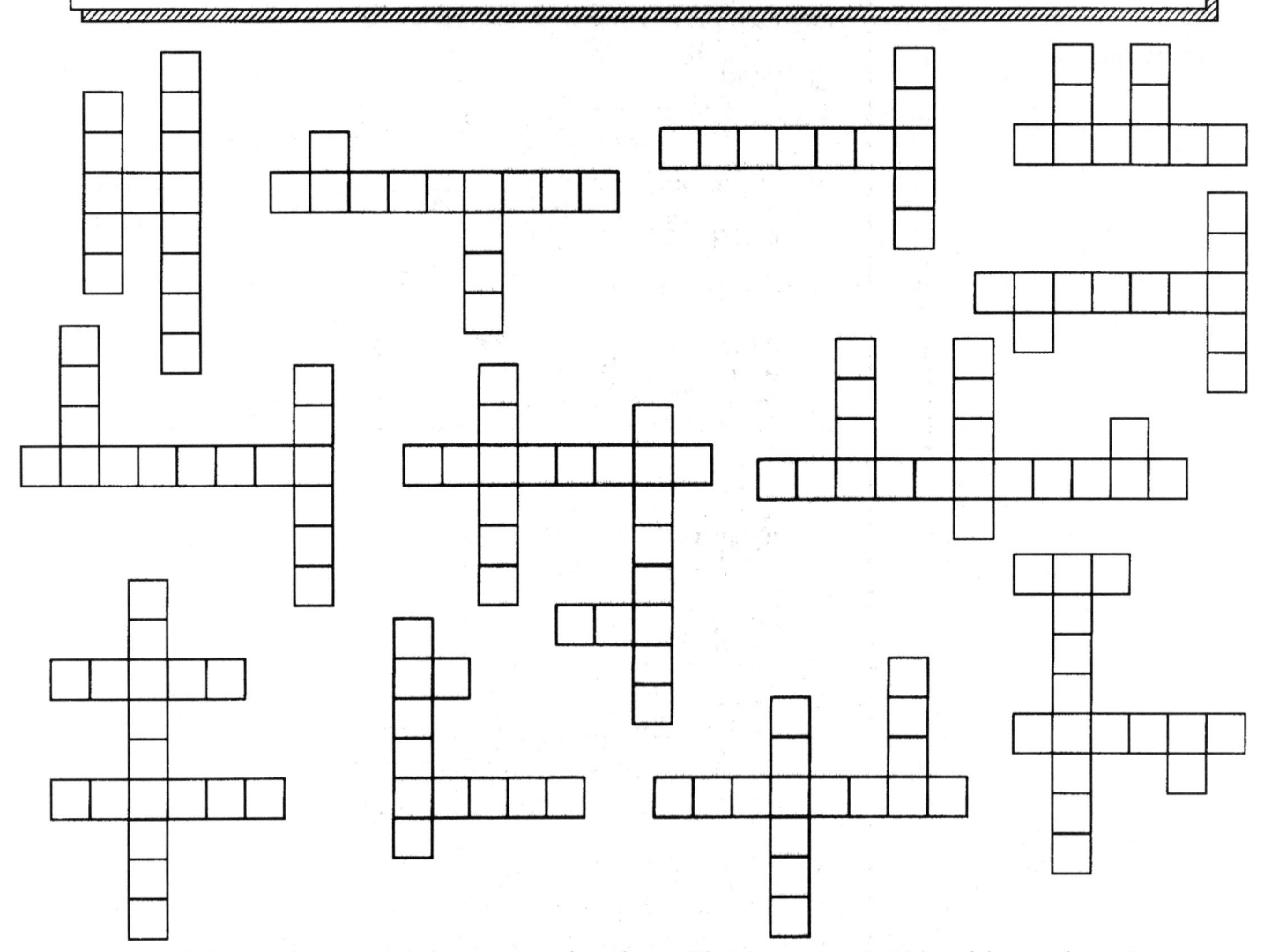

How many of these phrases can you remember from Christmas music? Would you dare sing a song to your class?

© Instructional Fair • TS Denison   IF8728 Challenge Your Mind

What Child Is This?

Name _____

Christmas

Fit the letters in each column into the boxes directly above them to form words. The letters may or may not go into the boxes in the same order in which they are given. Words may wrap to a second line. Your finished puzzle will describe one of the puzzles of the season. Ho, ho, ho!

A	T															
A̶	H	E	C	T	I	T	I	A	M	A	S	R	W	D	E	A	P
E	H	E	D	S	I	T	R	D	N	C	H	I	S	H	I	M	K
G	R	T		H	R	M	S	O	N	G	E		L	V	L	N	I
T	A̶				S	I		T		A			E			S	

"A CHRISTMAS CAROL" WAS FIRST PUBLISHED IN 1843. IT'S A DICKENS OF A STORY!

© Instructional Fair • TS Denison

IF8728 Challenge Your Mind

Christmas Superstitions in Threes

name _____

Three words are missing from each phrase. Match the letter of the missing phrase to each sentence.

____ 1. Holly placed in windows protects a ___ ___ ___ .

____ 2. A sprig of holly ___ ___ ___ brings happy dreams.

____ 3. Bells and chimes should be sounded on Christmas Day ___ ___ ___ evil spirits.

____ 4. A candle left burning all night in an empty room on Christmas Eve brings light, ___ ___ ___ all year.

____ 5. Anyone who is not kissed ___ ___ ___ will not marry during the next year.

____ 6. If Christmas bells toll on a Saturday, the winter will be foggy and the ___ ___ ___ .

____ 7. ___ ___ ___ on Christmas Day can tell the future.

____ 8. A cricket chirping at Christmas ___ ___ ___ .

____ 9. A stranger at the door on Christmas Eve may be ___ ___ ___ in disguise.

____ 10. On Christmas Eve ___ ___ ___ procession.

____ 11. Farm animals compare notes on how they've ___ ___ ___ in the past year.

____ 12. Ashes from ___ ___ ___ can cure many diseases.

____ 13. Bread baked on Christmas Eve will ___ ___ ___ .

____ 14. A green Christmas means ___ ___ ___ .

____ 15. A girl may knock on the gate of a pigsty. If a full-grown pig ___ ___ ___ she will marry an old man.

____ 16. People born the hour before midnight on Christmas Eve understand the ___ ___ ___ .

A. a person born
B. a white Easter
C. been treated during
D. brings good luck
E. following summer cold
F. grunts in reply
G. home from evil
H. language of animals
I. not become moldy
J. on the bedpost
K. sheep walk in
L. the Christ Child
M. the Yule log
N. to frighten away
O. under the mistletoe
P. warmth and plenty

© Instructional Fair • TS Denison

IF8728 Challenge Your Mind

Community Building

name _____

Kwanzaa

Fill in the blanks with words from the Word Box.

1. *Kwanzaa* is a word meaning "the first _____," It is based on the celebration of the gathering of crops in _____ countries.

2. Maulana Karenga, a _____ rights leader and teacher, introduced this community _____ to African Americans.

3. During Kwanzaa one pays _____ to one's _____ .

4. The principles of Kwanzaa emphasize working _____ for the sake of the whole community.

5. This celebration focuses on family and _____ , not religion.

6. Families may learn words in the Swahili _____ which was developed to _____ trade in East Africa.

7. On December 31 participants all gather for a *karamu*, or _____ .

8. On a low _____ is placed a *mkeka* which is a _____ mat.

9. The *kinara* or candle holder is _____ in the _____ of this *mkeka*.

10. Seven candles, one black, three red, and _____ green, are used in the *kinara*.

11. *Mazeo*, or fruits and _____ , may be set on the *mkeka* along with the *kikombe cha umoja*, or _____ cup.

12. A storyteller may share the _____ of the family and the _____ from Africa.

Word Box

African	feast	holiday	legends	together
ancestors	friends	honor	placed	unity
center	fruits	improve	table	vegetables
civil	history	language	three	woven

© Instructional Fair • TS Denison

IF8728 *Challenge Your Mind*

An African Tradition Returns

name _____

Kwanzaa

Nearly 5 million African Americans celebrate this festival focus on their cultural heritage.

Fit the letters in each column into the boxes directly above them to form words. The letters may or may not go into the boxes in the same order in which they are given. Words may wrap to a second line. Your finished puzzle will point out symbols of this Kwanzaa experience.

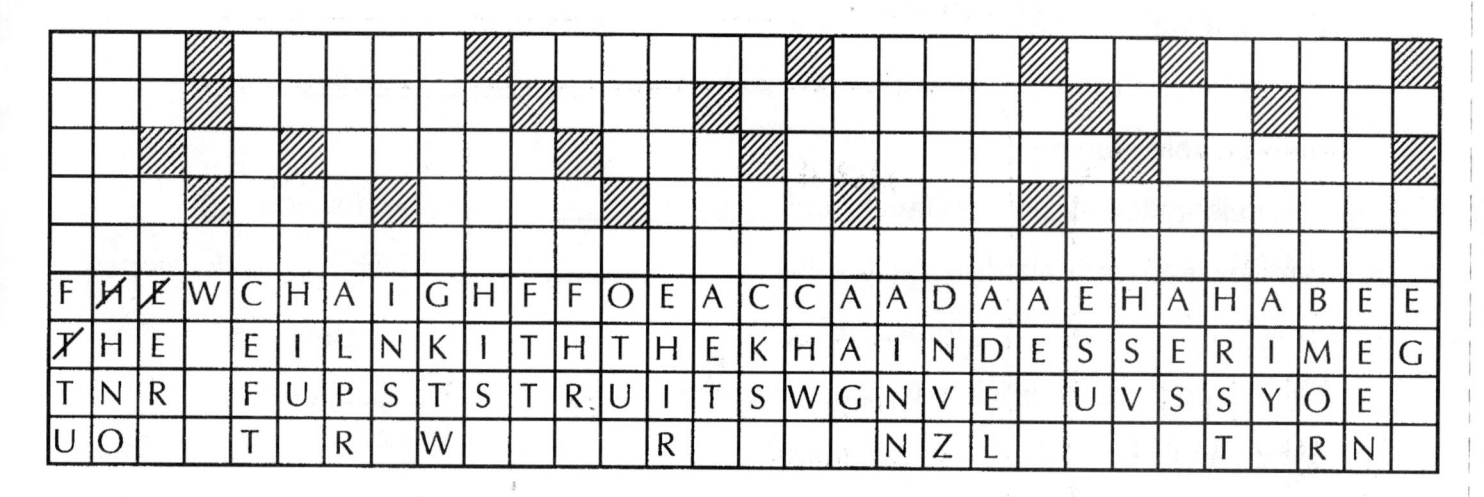

F	H	E	W	C	H	A	I	G	H	F	F	O	E	A	C	C	A	A	D	A	A	E	H	A	H	A	B	E	E
T	H	E		E	I	L	N	K	I	T	H	T	H	E	K	H	A	I	N	D	E	S	S	E	R	I	M	E	G
T	N	R		F	U	P	S	T	S	T	R	U	I	T	S	W	G	N	V	E		U	V	S	S	Y	O	E	
U	O			T		R		W					R						N	Z	L				T		R	N	

KWANZAA WAS ORIGINATED IN 1966 BY M. RON KARENGA. IT'S BASED ON A TRADITIONAL AFRICAN HARVEST FESTIVAL!

© Instructional Fair • TS Denison

IF8728 Challenge Your Mind

10 ... 9 ... 8 ...

name _____

New Year's Eve

The two lists below contain *partner* words. Match each word in List A with its partner in List B by drawing a straight line. As each line is drawn, it will pass through a bold-type letter. Set each of these letters in the blanks at the bottom of this page to finish this quatrain:

> As you behold this festive night
> With friends and kin so dear
> Do give your voice with all your might
> with shouts of _____ _____

MAYBE YOU'RE A POET AND DON'T KNOW IT!

List A
1. ball
2. fireworks
3. party
4. resolution
5. friendly
6. boisterous
7. group
8. radio
9. Father
10. counting
11. Auld
12. salted
13. hearty

List B
favors
games
down
fellowship
drop
Lang Syne
Time
toast
snacks
making
nostalgia
singing
display

Bold letters in grid: D M H I I H n C G E T E R

___ ___ ___ ___ ___ ___ ___ ___   ___ ___ ___ ___ ___
 1   2   3   4   5   6   7   8   9 10 11 12 13

© Instructional Fair • TS Denison

IF8728 *Challenge Your Mind*

Party Time

Unscramble these words and phrases to identify well known New Year's Day items.

1. big march of people and floats in California
   ttmnnaueor fo sorse erpdaa — **Tournament of Roses Parade**

2. a two-faced god from Roman mythology for whom we name this month
   saunj — **Janus**

3. a macho viewing which dominates this afternoon
   tlaoblof sgeam — **football games**

4. something often made in this merry season but seldom kept
   tssooiulren — **resolutions**

5. this is how the holiday begins in New York City
   labl pdor — **ball drop**

6. obnoxious non-musical instruments of noise
   rytap asrvfo — **party favors**

7. a sparkling display of sound and sight
   krreosifw — **fireworks**

8. a musical offering which memorializes the good old days
   dual ngal yens — **Auld Lang Syne**

9. beverage made of products from chicken, cow, and cane
   ogegng — **eggnog**

10. the Chinese New Year's Day, often later in year, celebrates this for each person
    ytiadrhb — **birthday**

Page 4

Bring on the New!

Fit the letters in each column into the boxes directly above them to form words. The letters may or may not go into the boxes in the same order in which they are given. Your finished puzzle is a translation from a Japanese poem about the new year.

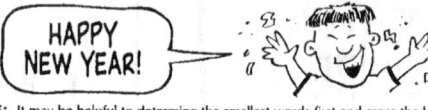

HOW MANY NIGHTS OH HOW
MANY NIGHTS TILL NEW YE
ARS DAY WHEN WE FLY OUR

KITES WHEN WE SPIN OU
R TOPS WHEN WE RUN AND
PLAY OH HOW MANY NIGH
TS TILL NEW YEARS DAY

HELPFUL HINTS: It may be helpful to determine the smallest words first and cross the letters off as you use them. Also, two words will wrap to a second line.

Page 5

It's the 12th Day!

January 6 is known as "the twelfth day of Christmas." In many places around the world, gifts are exchanged on this day to honor the memory of the gifts of the Wise Men, long ago. Here are the twelve gifts from the song *The Twelve Days of Christmas*. Can you determine the code and decipher the names of the presents?

a. GOLDEN RINGS
b. PIPERS PIPING
c. MAIDS AMILKING
d. FRENCH HENS
e. PARTRIDGE IN A PEAR TREE
f. LORDS ALEAPING
g. TURTLE DOVES
h. GEESE ALAYING
i. LADIES DANCING
j. DRUMMERS DRUMMING
k. CALLING BIRDS
l. SWANS ASWIMMING

Gifts
swans a-swimming
maids a-milking
calling birds
turtle doves
drummers drumming
lords a-leaping
French hens
partridge in a pear tree
golden rings
ladies dancing
geese a-laying
pipers piping

CODE
A	B	C	D	E	F	G	H	I	J	K	L	M
Y	O	D	U	L	G	A	W	P		I	E	N

N	O	P	Q	R	S	T	U	V	W	X	Y	Z
S		C	M	T	F		R	K		V	B	

Page 6

Name the Author

This 17th century writer is best known for the fairy tales he wrote. He also compiled a book of *Mother Goose* rhymes before the English did. To find his name, figure out the titles or first lines of each rhyme. He authored versions of the four stories, but the eleven rhymes are ancient lore with uncertain origins.

1. an accident-prone H₂O-obtaining pair on a tumble
2. an oval unborn chick topples and breaks his shell
3. a wool producer of dark hue who bleats
4. a maiden with minuscule feet who reposes by the fire
5. a happy monarch requests his comforts—including some tobacco
6. a frustrated mother who lives in a leather home begets too many offspring
7. a wise, galoshes-wearing feline
8. this barnyard thief is the son of a flautist
9. a feline violinist is joined by a menagerie and tableware
10. a Halloween gourd chomper
11. a trusting child strolls off to visit her sick grandmother
12. a gorgeous lass who befriends some little people gets smooched
13. three merchants floating in an open barrel
14. a dairy products sipper is appalled by a friendly arachnid
15. five petite porkers

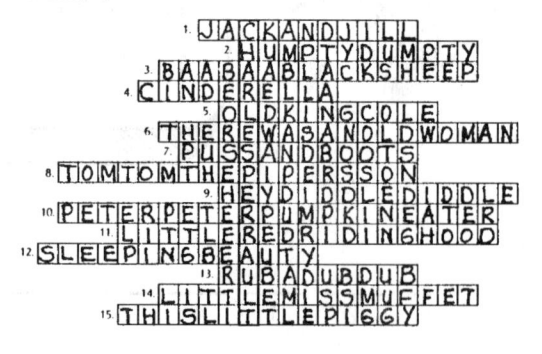

1. JACKANDJILL
2. HUMPTYDUMPTY
3. BAABAABLACKSHEEP
4. CINDERELLA
5. OLDKINGCOLE
6. THEREWASANOLDWOMAN
7. PUSSANDBOOTS
8. TOMTOMTHEPIPERSSON
9. HEYDIDDLEDIDDLE
10. PETERPETERPUMPKINEATER
11. LITTLEREDRIDINGHOOD
12. SLEEPINGBEAUTY
13. RUBADUBDUB
14. LITTLEMISSMUFFET
15. THISLITTLEPIGGY

Page 7

Hello, Pooh!

Fill in the diagram with the words listed to form a quotation from A. A. Milne's *Winnie the Pooh*. The quotation will read from left to right. Included are letters to assist you.

What does Pooh say while knocking on Rabbit's door?

A.A. MILNE ALSO WROTE "THE RED HOUSE MYSTERY" IN 1921!

Word List
be	isn't	rabbit	that
because	must	said	there
hallo	must	somebody	there
have	nobody	somebody	you

T	H	E	R	E	M	U	S	T	B
E	S	O	M	E	B	O	D	Y	T
H	E	R	E	B	E	C	A	U	S
E	S	O	M	E	B	O	D	Y	M
U	S	T	H	A	V	E	S	A	I
D	N	O	B	O	D	Y	H	A	L
L	O	R	A	B	B	I	T	I	S
N	T	T	H	A	T	Y	O	U	?

Hint: Some words will wrap to the next line.

The Gentleman General

Discover facts about the remarkable soldier Robert E. Lee. The letters in the bold boxes of the completed puzzle will tell you even more. Use an encyclopedia or other information source if you're stumped.

1. In July of 1863, his army was forced to leave this Pennsylvania town.
2. At this battle, Lee had his greatest success and greatest loss.
3. This is the war for which Lee is most well-known.
4. The name of the South's president was Jefferson _____.
5. Lee's wife was the great granddaughter of _____ (Curtis) Washington.
6. This was Lee's army rank.
7. The Southern states formed this union.
8. After the war Lee became president of _____ College (it now includes his name).
9. Here Lee commanded the Federal troops as they subdued John Brown's raid.
10. Lee's dad, Henry, was a cavalry officer nicknamed "Light _____ _____."
11. He served as officer in this war alongside General Scott.
12. This is the state Lee served faithfully.
13. Lee's great friend who died serving him, was _____ Jackson.
14. Lee's father fought in this war.
15. Lee received his training at this school.

ROBERT E. LEE WAS BORN ON JANUARY 19, 1807!

HIS FATHER WAS "LIGHT HORSE HARRY" LEE!

1. GETTYSBURG
2. CHANCELLORSVILLE
3. CIVILWAR
4. DAVIS
5. MARTHA
6. GENERAL
7. CONFEDERACY
8. WASHINGTON
9. HARPERSFERRY
10. HORSEHARRY
11. MEXICANWAR
12. VIRGINIA
13. STONEWALL
14. REVOLUTIONARY
15. WESTPOINT

I Have a Dream Today

Unscramble the bold faced letters below to complete words from this segment of Martin Luther King's famous speech.

When we let **DEEFMOR** FREEDOM ring, when we let it **GINR** RING from every **AEGILLV** VILLAGE and every hamlet, from every state and every **YITC** CITY, we will be able to **DEPES** SPEED up that day when all of God's **CDEHILNR** CHILDREN, **ABCKL** BLACK men and white men, **SEJW** JEWS and **EEGILNST** GENTILES, **AENOPRSSTTT** PROTESTANTS and Catholics, will be **LAEB** ABLE to join hands and sing in the **DORSW** WORDS of the old Negro **UAIILPRST** SPIRITUAL, "Free at last! **EFER** FREE at last! Thank God **TAGYHILM** ALMIGHTY, we **RAE** ARE free at last!"

MARTIN LUTHER KING, JR. RECEIVED A BACHELOR'S DEGREE IN SOCIOLOGY FROM MOREHOUSE COLLEGE IN 1948!

We Are the Champions!

Early and his teammates won the all-school co-ed basketball tournament in Hoosierville, Indinoisigan. (Ever hear of it?) Early's male teammates are Arvell and Derek. The straight-shooting girl teammates are Fiona, Bonnie, and Carly. No two players scored the same number of points nor committed the same number of fouls although one player did foul out. Use the clues below to match each player with the points scored and the fouls committed.

Hint: Once you record a yes (y) in a box, write no (n) in all the boxes in that row and column.

Clues:
1. The girl who scored nine points had no fouls. Derek had four points and an even number of fouls.
2. Fiona scored more points than Bonnie who scored one more point than a boy. This boy outscored another teammate.
3. Two girls closed with the highest scores. They had either 2 or 5 fouls.
4. The 11-point male closed with 3 fouls. Carly scored the most points.
5. Fiona had one less foul than Early.

I DON'T THINK THE BULLS HAVE ANYTHING TO WORRY ABOUT!

Team	Points Scored						Fouls Committed					
	4	8	9	11	12	14	0	1	2	3	4	5
Arvell		X										
Bonnie												
Carly					X							X
Derek	X											
Early											X	
Fiona												

© Instructional Fair • TS Denison

IF8728 *Challenge Your Mind*

Wade in the Water, Children

Name _____

Here are the names of 20 important black Americans. Match each one with his or her description.

Name List

Bill Cosby			
Rosa Parks	Mohammed Ali	Shirley Chisholm	Langston Hughes
W.E.B. DuBois	Jesse Jackson	Tom Bradley	Spike Lee
Martin Luther King	L. Douglas Wilder	Leontyne Price	Jackie Robinson
Malcolm X	Thurgood Marshall	Guion S. Bluford	Booker T. Washington

1. first black in professional baseball
2. a founder of the N.A.A.C.P
3. first black Supreme Court justice
4. early female black representative in U.S. House
5. first black mayor of Los Angeles
6. ran in presidential primary in '84
7. comedian and television sit-com star
8. first black astronaut in space
9. early black educator; preached patience
10. Baptist minister; preached non-violence
11. black Muslim leader who called for a social revolution
12. refused to give up her bus seat
13. filmmaker
14. a Harlem Renaissance poet
15. female opera singer
16. first black governor
17. sting-like-a-butterfly boxer

1. JACKIEROBINSON
2. WEBDUBOIS
3. THURGOODMARSHALL
4. SHIRLEYCHISHOLM
5. TOMBRADLEY
6. JESSEJACKSON
7. BILLCOSBY
8. GUIONSBLUFORD
9. BOOKERTWASHINGTON
10. MARTINLUTHERKING
11. MALCOLMX
12. ROSAPARKS
13. SPIKELEE
14. LANGSTONHUGHES
15. LEONTYNEPRICE
16. LDOUGLASWILDER
17. MOHAMMEDALI

Page 12

Wake Up!

Name _____

Insert the 22 letters from the letter bank into the empty boxes to form words relating to the groundhog. The letter you insert may be the first, the last, or in the middle of the word. Cross out letters in the letter bank as you use them. Note: Not all letters in each row are used to form words! The completed puzzle will state a fact about this furry creature.

Hidden message: THE WOODCHUCK HIBERNATES

"KEEP IT DOWN, WILL YA?! I'M TRYING TO GET SOME SLEEP HERE!!"

Letter Bank

A B C C D E E E
H H H I K N O O
R S T T U W

Page 13

A Wild Carnival

Name _____

Mardi Gras is a festive holiday with a very old history. Its celebration combines aspects of Christian, ancient Egyptian, and Roman traditions.

Match each word from the Word Box to its definition. The letter boxes may help you do this more easily.

Word Box

band	dancers	fat Tuesday	masquerade	Rex	parades
carne vale	Epiphany	float	New Orleans	Shrovetide	
costume	Fast Nacht	pageantry	Pancake Day		

1. "farewell meat"
2. the U.S. center for this holiday festival
3. to pretend or to disguise oneself
4. the fanciful clothing of a Mardi Gras reviler
5. the French translation of "Mardi Gras"
6. those whose body movements follow a pattern of rhythm and music
7. the German name for this day; also the name for its rectangular doughnuts
8. a company of musicians
9. the 3 days of confession for past sins
10. the English name for this day; a time to dispense with eggs, milk, and fat
11. a low, flat-topped car/wagon used in parades
12. holy day that begins this season
13. king of the New Orleans carnival
14. a splendid display of pomp
15. huge, colorful processions in this festival

1. carnevale
2. NewOrleans
3. masquerade
4. costume
5. FatTuesday
6. dancers
7. FastNacht
8. band
9. Shrovetide
10. PancakeDay
11. float
12. Epiphany
13. Rex
14. pageantry
15. parades

Page 14

Brand Spankin' New

Name _____

February 11 has been named Inventors Day in honor of Thomas Edison's birthday. For each inventor you'll find letters encircling the name. Use these letters to discover what the person invented.

- Robert Fulton — steamboat
- Jacques Cousteau — Aqua Lung
- Ladislao Biro — ballpoint pen
- Sergei Korolev — space rocket
- Johan Vaaler — safety pin
- Nikolaus Otto — 4-cylinder gas engine
- John Harington — flush toilet
- Garrett Morgan — traffic light
- Chester Carlson — photocopier
- Thomas Edison — phonograph
- Evangelista Torricelli — barometer
- Dennis Gabor — hologram
- Chester Greenwood — earmuffs
- Samuel Morse — telegraph
- J.B.L. Foucault — gyroscope

Page 15

Honest Abe

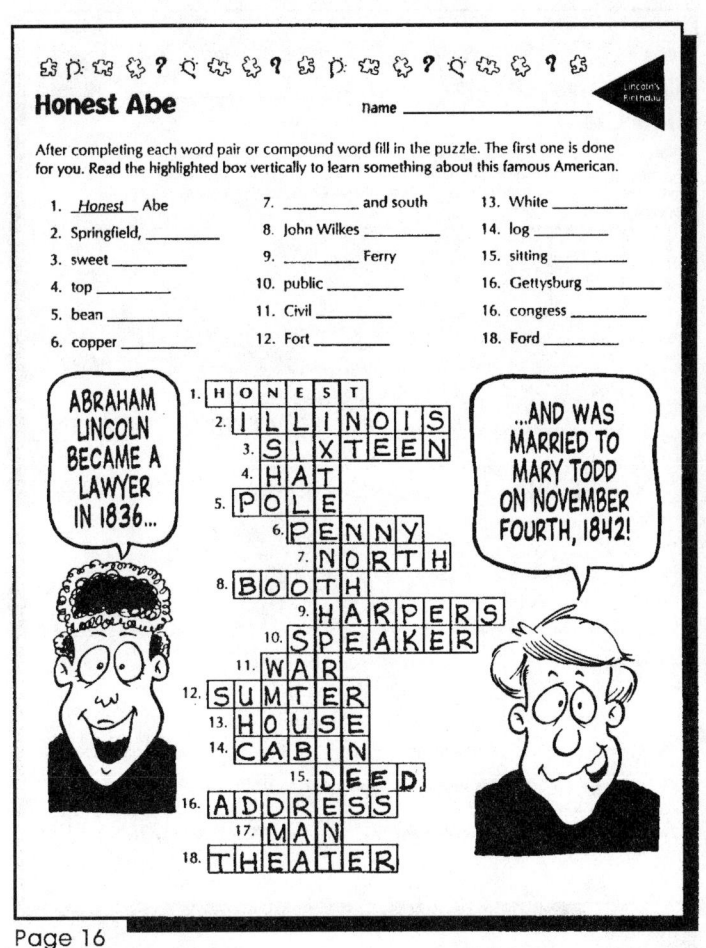

After completing each word pair or compound word fill in the puzzle. The first one is done for you. Read the highlighted box vertically to learn something about this famous American.

1. _Honest_ Abe
2. Springfield, _____
3. sweet _____
4. top _____
5. bean _____
6. copper _____
7. _____ and south
8. John Wilkes _____
9. _____ Ferry
10. public _____
11. Civil _____
12. Fort _____
13. White _____
14. log _____
15. sitting _____
16. Gettysburg _____
16. congress _____
18. Ford _____

ABRAHAM LINCOLN BECAME A LAWYER IN 1836...

1. HONEST
2. ILLINOIS
3. SIXTEEN
4. HAT
5. POLE
6. PENNY
7. NORTH
8. BOOTH
9. HARPERS
10. SPEAKER
11. WAR
12. SUMTER
13. HOUSE
14. CABIN
15. DEED
16. ADDRESS
17. MAN
18. THEATER

...AND WAS MARRIED TO MARY TODD ON NOVEMBER FOURTH, 1842!

Page 16

Hail to the Chief

Find out about two U.S. presidents. To solve the puzzles, write the name of each picture. Use the numbers below the spaces to help you solve each president's "formula."

WHIP LEAVES DOOR
18 11 15 6 1 22 12 5 21 8 4 16 13 9

TENT FEET
19 2 17 10 3 14 7 20

Franklin D. Roosevelt

HE WAS THE FIRST
11 22 18 12 8 20 11 14 3 15 9 8 10

PRESIDENT ON TELEVISION
6 9 28 8 15 4 22 17 10 3 17 19 7 15 5 15 8 15 16 17

THEODORE ROOSEVELT WAS THE FIRST PRESIDENT OF THE TWENTIETH CENTURY... ...WHO IS THE LAST?

BEAR STAR PENCIL CANDLE
13 29 6 11 24 17 5 11 17 1 28 21 2 14 5 4 19 8

HOG TWO
14 10 22 20 5 26

James Garfield

THE LAST PRESIDENT BORN
24 14 8 17 5 20 4 25 18 15 13 26 7 18

IN A LOG CABIN
21 1 6 19 10 22 12 5 13 21 18

Page 17

The Beautiful Voice

Fill in the blanks using choices from the Word Bank to learn more about this great singer.

Word Bank
arranged, at, before, black, Eisenhower, hall, inauguration, Memorial, Metropolitan, once, people, perform, permitted, remarked, steps, Toscanini, voice, when, years, York

Marian Anderson was the first **black** singer to **perform** at the **Metropolitan** Opera House in New **York** City. She sang for Arturo **Toscanini**. He **remarked** that she had "a **voice** that comes only **once** in a hundred **years**." In 1939, **when** Anderson was not **permitted** to sing **at** one music **hall**, Eleanor Roosevelt **arranged** for her to sing **before** 75,000 **people** outdoors on the **steps** of the Lincoln **Memorial**. She sang at the **inauguration** balls of both Presidents **Eisenhower** and Kennedy. She died in 1993 at the age of 91.

Write eight words to describe singing voices using the letters of Ms. Anderson's surname.
ANSWERS WILL VARY.

A _____
N _____
D _____
E _____
R _____
S _____
O _____
N _____

MARIAN ANDERSON RECEIVED A KENNEDY CENTER HONOR IN 1978!

Page 18

Hey, No Lie!

Combine letter groups to complete words that fit the phrases below. The first one is done for you. It will help to cross off letter groups as you use them.

1. Washington's nickname — _Father of His Country_
2. colony in which Washington was born — Virginia
3. the peace-time profession for which George received training — Surveyor
4. Washington's plantation estate — Mount Vernon
5. the wife of Washington — Martha Custis
6. America's struggle against Great Britain — Revolution
7. what Americans hoped to receive from Great Britain — independence
8. In 1876, Congress granted Washington this highest military title — General
9. the political organization which elected him as its presiding officer was the Constitutional — convention
10. Washington took this office in 1789 — presidency

Letter Groups

a	fa	of	tion
al	gen	or	tion
con	gi	pen	tis
coun	his	pre	try
cus	lu	re	ven
cy	mar	si	ver
de	mou	sur	vey
den	ni	tha	vir
dence	non	ther	vo
er	nt		

GEORGE WASHINGTON WAS APPOINTED SURVEYOR OF CULPEPPER COUNTY IN 1749 AND THAT'S THE TRUTH!

Page 19

© Instructional Fair • TS Denison

IF8728 Challenge Your Mind

Revealed by Gabriel

Use context clues to fill in the blanks below with words from the Word Bank.

Word Bank

angel	careful	greediness	Muslims	shifts
based	closes	greetings	new	sip
calendar	during	holy	revelations	sunrise
called	feast	month	sent	

OBSERVANCE OF THE FAST IS ONE OF THE FIVE PILLARS OF ISLAM!

1. *Ramadan* is the ninth month of the *Islamic* calendar. Ramadan honors the time when the **angel** Gabriel made **revelations** to *Muhammad*.
2. **Muslims** believe that God **sent** down the *Koran* during this month.
3. The *Koran* is the most **holy** book of the *Islamic* faith.
4. *Muslims* fast from **sunrise** to sunset during this entire month.
5. They may not even have a **sip** of water **during** this daytime fast.
6. During Ramadan one must be most **careful**. Lying, slandering, and **greediness** may undo the penance of the fast.
7. A three-day festival **called** *'Id al-Fitr* **closes** this month.
8. During this **feast** families gather to pray and give gifts to one another.
9. *Muslims* celebrate the closing feast with **new** clothes and warm **greetings** for each other.
10. Each year the **month** of *Ramadan* **shifts** backward eleven days on the Roman calendar because the *Muslim* holidays are **based** on the lunar **calendar**.

Page 20

Celebrating the New Life

Different cultures around the world have unique ways of celebrating the newness of springtime. For many people spring means the beginning of the new year. Depending on the cultural group this may begin sometime between late January and early May. Use the code to translate the words into readable English.

1. the Iranian spring festival — **NOWRUZ**
2. in Iran, each family member would jump this to ask for a good luck blessing — **BONFIRE**
3. the Iranian festival lasts this many days — **THIRTEEN**
4. the Thai water festival marking the start of the Buddhist new year — **SONGKRAN**
5. this is sprayed over crowds by enormous statues of Buddah — **PERFUME**
6. until 1752 this holiday was celebrated on March 25 in England — **NEW YEARS**
7. a "stinking idol" to the Puritans — **MAY POLE**
8. on this day Christians celebrate victory of life over death — **EASTER**
9. Vietnamese new year festival — **TET**
10. legendary beast of good fortune in Vietnam — **UNICORN**
11. at this festival Vietnamese pay respect to these people — **ANCESTORS**
12. it celebrates Hebrew freedom from slavery — **PASSOVER**

Page 21

When a Girl Saved Her People

During Purim, Jews around the world recall how Esther, a beautiful Jewish-girl-turned-Persian queen, protected her people from annihilation. Her uncle Mordecai had once saved King Xerxes' life by uncovering a plot to assassinate the monarch. For this, Xerxes richly rewarded the uncle. The evil noble Haman in jealous hatred wanted Mordecai killed. He persuaded the monarch to pass an edict which called for the execution of all Jews in the empire. However, the brave princess, at a private banquet for the king and Haman, spoiled the cruel lord's plans when she informed them both that she too was a Jew. Haman was hung from the gallows he erected for Mordecai, and the Jewish citizens living in Persia did not die.

Unscramble the letters below to match each definition given.

Definition	Scrambled Letters	Answer
1. place of hangings	WOGLASL	GALLOWS
2. a law	DETIC	EDICT
3. a king	NMAHORC	MONARCH
4. a special dinner	TAQENBU	BANQUET
5. to remember	LACERL	RECALL
6. to murder a famous person	SNASIESTASA	ASSASSINATE
7. former name of Iran	SPAIRE	PERSIA
8. to be covetous	SUOLAJE	JEALOUS
9. to ruin	LOPIS	SPOIL
10. father's brother	NLECU	UNCLE
11. destruction	LINIHOITANNA	ANNIHILATION
12. to convince	UREAPEDS	PERSUADE

Page 22

Rock-A-Bye

Fit the letters in each column into the boxes directly above them to form words. The letters may or may not go into the boxes in the same order in which they are given. Your finished puzzle will show a lullaby for a baby taken from a poem by Sir Walter Scott.

OH HUSH THEE MY BABY THY SIRE WAS A KNIGHT THY MOTHER A LADY BOTH LOVELY AND BRIGHT THE WOOD AND THE

GLENS FROM THE TOWERS WHICH WE SEE THEY ALL ARE BELONGING DEAR BABY TO THEE

HELPFUL HINTS: Sir Walter Scott would have used an old English spelling for baby, but we used a contemporary spelling. Some words may wrap to a second line.

Page 23

© Instructional Fair • TS Denison

IF8728 Challenge Your Mind

Go Gaelic!

Ar choimrí' Dé' go raibh gach duine da'r gcairde
agus sonas go dtuga Se' go fial do'ibhsean agus du'inne in Eirinn.

This Gaelic quotation was made on St. Patrick's Day by the Irish president Eamon de Valera more than 30 years ago. To translate it into English, fill in the letter boxes with words from the Word Box.

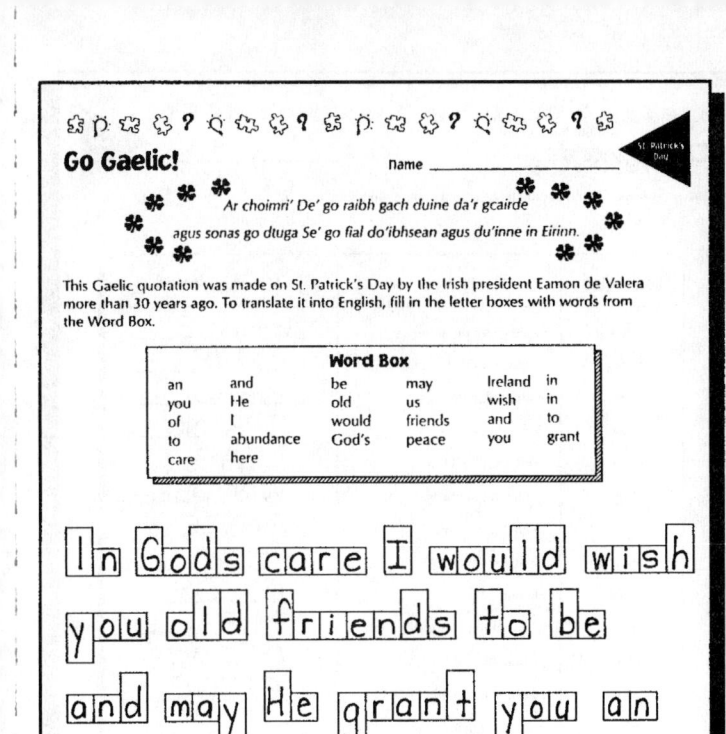

Word Box

an	and	be	may	Ireland	in
you	He	old	us	wish	in
of	I	would	friends	and	to
to	abundance	God's	peace	you	grant
care	here				

In God's care I would wish you old friends to be and may He grant you an abundance of peace and to us here in Ireland

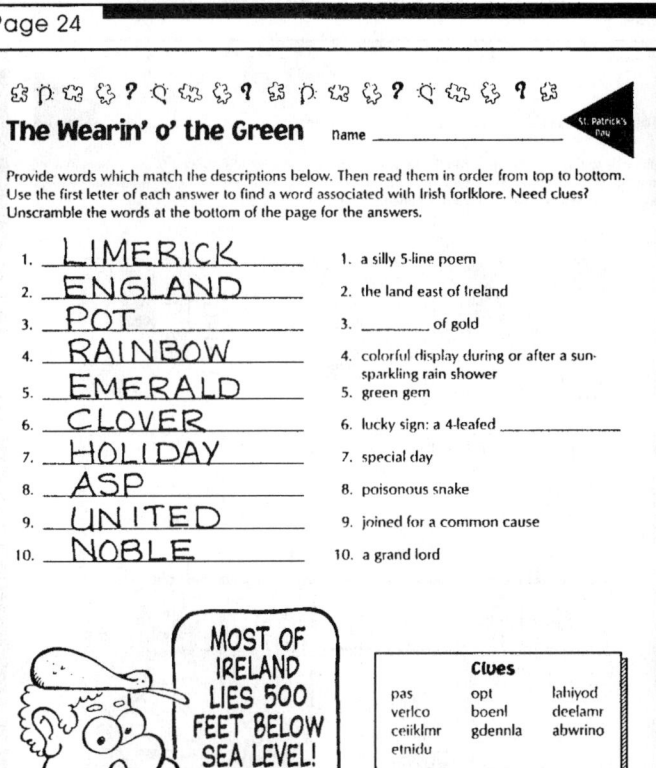

Page 24

Th' Luck o' the Irish

Decipher the names of these Saint Paddy's Day terms. The first letter of each object pictured is the letter that is written on each line.

1. S N A K E
2. S T P A T R I C K
3. G R E E N
4. S H A M R O C K
5. L E P R E C H A U N

Challenge—Now design your own picture puzzles for these five terms:

Gaelic   Potato Famine   Limerick   Independence   James Joyce

Page 25

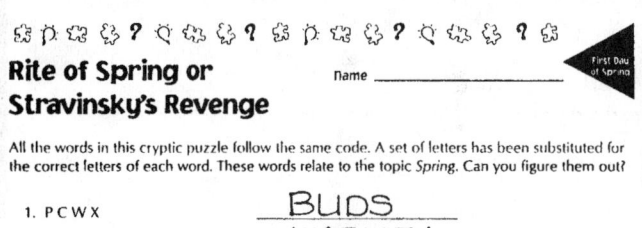

The Wearin' o' the Green

Provide words which match the descriptions below. Then read them in order from top to bottom. Use the first letter of each answer to find a word associated with Irish folklore. Need clues? Unscramble the words at the bottom of the page for the answers.

1. LIMERICK — a silly 5-line poem
2. ENGLAND — the land east of Ireland
3. POT — _____ of gold
4. RAINBOW — colorful display during or after a sun-sparkling rain shower
5. EMERALD — green gem
6. CLOVER — lucky sign: a 4-leafed _____
7. HOLIDAY — special day
8. ASP — poisonous snake
9. UNITED — joined for a common cause
10. NOBLE — a grand lord

MOST OF IRELAND LIES 500 FEET BELOW SEA LEVEL! AYE AND BEGORRAH!

Clues

pas	opt	lahiyod
verlco	boenl	deelamr
ceiiklrm	gdennla	abwrino
etnidu		

Page 26

Rite of Spring or Stravinsky's Revenge

All the words in this cryptic puzzle follow the same code. A set of letters has been substituted for the correct letters of each word. These words relate to the topic *Spring*. Can you figure them out?

1. PCWX — BUDS
2. VYTOJK — WARMTH
3. RGXUIJX — INSECTS
4. XKQVUTX — SHOWERS
5. OQVRGS — MOWING
6. AEQVUTX — FLOWERS
7. PRTWXQGS — BIRDSONG
8. HEYGJRGS — PLANTING
9. USSX — EGGS
10. STUUG — GREEN
11. PEQXXQOX — BLOSSOMS
12. PRTJK — BIRTH
13. TQPRGX — ROBINS
14. XUUWX — SEEDS
15. XCGXKRGU — SUNSHINE

CLUES:
1. The letter X represents S.
2. The letter Q represents O.
3. The letter S represents G.
4. The letter G represents N.

IGOR STRAVINSKY WAS A LAW STUDENT BEFORE HE BEGAN TO STUDY MUSICAL COMPOSITION!

Page 27

© Instructional Fair • TS Denison

IF8728 *Challenge Your Mind*

Spring Madness

Three girls and two boys, ages 9 to 14, each perform some activity on this special religious holiday weekend. See if you can match each one with his or her age and activity.

Clues:
1. The ten-year-old girl, Ogden, and the seeder, are three different people.
2. The boy who goes to Mass is younger than Mary.
3. The eldest student bought new clothes for this holiday.
4. Petra is younger than the female seeder who is younger than Ogden.
5. Leo, who is not the nine-year-old egg-painter, is younger than 12 but older than Petra.
6. Nadia, who did not celebrate Passover, is not 12.
7. The youngest student is not Petra and does not celebrate Passover.

	celebrates Passover	seeds flower bed	buys clothes	attends Mass	paints Easter eggs	9	10	11	12	14
Leo				X				X		
Mary		X							X	
Nadia				X	X					
Ogden			X							X
Petra	X									

PETRA WAS THE CAPITAL OF NABATAEA FROM 400 B.C. TO 200 A.D..REALLY!

Page 28

Easter Words

Write the words in the Word List next to the synonyms they match.

Word List	Related Words	Matching Word
cross	charity, mercy, leniency	GRACE
spring	animate, vital, existing	ALIVE
grave	cottontail, hare	RABBIT
flower	vernal, seedtime	SPRING
green	vault, hurdle, jump	LEAP
smile	amazement, marveling	WONDER
leap	beam, grin	SMILE
miracle	blossom, floret, bloom	FLOWER
rabbit	crucifix	CROSS
grow	phenomenon, wonderment	MIRACLE
alive	propagate, cultivate, produce	GROW
burst	tomb, mausoleum, crypt	GRAVE
grace	ascent, mount	ARISE
wonder	verdant, fresh, new	GREEN
arise	flourish, explode	BURST

Page 29

Homophonic Homily

Complete the Easter story with words from the word list. As you determine each word, place it in the crossword. Use each word only once.

Word Pair List
- altar/alter
- brake/break
- feat/feet
- grate/great
- groan/grown
- hair/hare
- knew/new
- rite/write
- threw/through
- watt/what

Believe it or not, one day we had to **brake** (1) for a four-foot-tall white rabbit carrying an Easter basket. His name was Harvey. As he thanked us for avoiding his demise, Harvey showed us his **great** (2) big basket filled with chocolates, eggs, and various objects of springtime affection. Then he told us his story.

One Easter I foolishly fought with my sister Harmony. On that day long ago I **threw** (3) four painted eggs at her. But not all of the eggs would **break** (4). No, indeed! I missed with three finely painted eggs which slipped through a **grate** (5) in the street in front of our house. I was filled with remorse. My parents would scold me for hitting my sister, and I lost three of our precious creations. Loudly did I **groan** (6) for I **knew** (7) I would never see these eggs again. As Harmony tried to comb the eggy mess out of her **hair** (8) she wailed, "**What** (9) have you done? You are a mean-spirited monster of a **hare** (10)!" Then she scurried off to our warren to **alter** (11) her appearance.

"I remained outdoors, afraid to pass before my parents. As I stalled the arrival of my certain punishment, I saw movement behind the grate. I peeked **through** (12) the metal frame. Oh, I had **grown** (13) much the past winter, and I needed to squeeze to enter the sewer. Down the line I saw a dim light. A 40-**watt** (14) bulb was suspended from a wall. Before an **altar** (15) made of stone and pebble stood an aged groundhog. He appeared to be performing some strange **rite** (16) of spring. A **new** (17) brilliantly flowered Easter hat sat on his wide furry head. He solemnly turned toward me and said, "Be sure to **write** (18) about all you see here."

But this, alas, is too great a **feat** (19) for one of my folk. I have never written with my fore **feet**. (20)

HAY, WATT'S GNU?

Page 30

Whiz-Dumb?

Fit the letters in each column into the boxes directly above them to form words. The letters may or may not go into the boxes in the same order in which they are given. Your completed puzzle is a proverb for this day. The first word is done for you.

I	T		I	S		A		W	I	S	E		F
O	O	L		W	H	O		H	I	D	E	S		H
I	S		I	G	N	O	R	A	N	C	E		I	N
S	I	L	E	N	T		B	L	I	S	S			

O	S	L	I	E	H	T	A	A	L	D	E	E	I	H
I	O	/	L	I	N	O	R	B	W	C	E	S		N
/	I		W	S	O		H	N	I	S	S	S		F
S			G	N					I	S				

I'M A LITTLE CONFUSED!

Hint: Some words may wrap to a second line.

Page 31

Treed Me Right!

On Arbor Day many people make a habit of planting a tree. Can you plant a tree in your mind? Use the letter diagrams to name 25 trees.

[Code grid: A B C / D E F / G H I | J K L / M N O / P Q R | S T U / V | W X Y / Z]

1. Sweet Gum
2. Elm
3. Birch
4. Eucalyptus
5. Red Pine
6. Sitka Spruce
7. Cottonwood
8. Douglas Fir
9. Larch
10. Juniper
11. Pin Oak
12. Rosewood
13. Mahogany
14. Ash
15. Redwood
16. Walnut
17. Beech
18. Cedar
19. Hickory
20. Teak
21. Sequoia

Arbor Day

Page 32

A Toast to Critters

Determine as many words as you can in the *Words* column. Then transfer these letters onto the *Solution* blanks with the same number code. You will have a poem by E.V. Rieu.

Definitions	Words
a large oceanic mammal	W H A L E (1-5)
an enormous American reptile; luggage skin	A L L I G A T O R (6-14)
an African ape that climbs well	C H I M P A N Z E E (15-24)
a nocturnal, winged insect that produces its own light.	F I R E F L Y (25-31)
a waterfowl of Donald fame	D U C K (32-35)
a great, antlered mammal of the North American forest	M O O S E (36-40)

Solution:

THE HAPPINESS OF HEDGEHOGS
LIES IN COMPLETE REPOSE. THEY
SPEND THE MONTHS OF WINTER IN
A LONG DELICIOUS DOZE; AND IF
THEY NOTE THE TIME AT ALL THEY
THINK "HOW FAST IT GOES!"

Page 33

Giving to Caesar

Who says this is a holiday? Probably not adults. But if you play it right, you may be able to convince your folks to go out to eat . . . just to celebrate the completion of their taxes.

Find the List Words in the wordsearch below. The six unused letters in the puzzle will spell out a word in the end.

List Words

tax return, alien, income, above, deduction, cash, benefit, gift, family, call, bond, busy, residence, local, send, interest, self, limit, land, join, note, loser, amount, status, refund, home, late, social security, federal, adjustment, less, real estate, pain, revenue, cent, internal, report, exempt, nervous, joint

PAYDAY

Tax Day

TAXATION WAS ONE OF THE MAIN CAUSES OF THE REVOLUTIONARY WAR!

Page 34

On to Lexington!

This day is celebrated especially in parts of Massachusetts and Maine. It honors patriots of the American Revolution. Use the Letter List to add a letter to each word. Then rearrange the letters to form words about the patriots.

Letter List: C C C C E H I I K N N O R R R S T T T X

WORD	Letter	New Word	Hint
1. boost	N	BOSTON	MA city
2. slider	O	SOLDIER	redcoat
3. lives	R	SILVER	precious metals
4. die	R	RIDE	to be carried along
5. rental	N	LANTERN	old light
6. sore	H	HORSE	mare or filly
7. loony	C	COLONY	one of 13
8. real	T	ALERT	to warn
9. bleat	T	BATTLE	larger than a skirmish
10. rot	Y	TORY	British loyalist
11. cordon	C	CONCORD	town of early battle
12. mutes	K	MUSKET	old-fashioned gun
13. harm	C	MARCH	military walk
14. pasture	C	CAPTURES	seizes
15. arbor	H	HARBOR	port
16. sort	T	TROTS	prances
17. thou	S	SHOUT	yell
18. sine	R	REINS	straps of a horse's bit
19. lathe	R	HALTER	horse's lead rope
20. teas	X	TAXES	money for the IRS

Patriot Day

Page 35

© Instructional Fair • TS Denison

IF8728 *Challenge Your Mind*

All Is Mended

Below are quotes from five of William Shakespeare's great plays. Unscramble the name of each speaker and fill in the name of each play. May the world be your stage.

1. The pound of flesh which I demand of him
   is dearly bought, is mine, and I will have it. (IV.i.99)   chklosy **Shylock**
   Play: eth ancremht fo icnvee   **THE MERCHANT OF VENICE**

2. When we are born, we cry that we are come
   To this great stage of fools. (IV.vi.182-183)   aelr **Lear**
   Play: ainrlgke **KING LEAR**

3. My hour is almost come,
   When I to sulf'rous and tormenting flames
   Must render up myself. (I.iv. 3-5)   tsohg **Ghost**
   Play: lemhat **HAMLET**

4. If we shadows have offended,
   Think but this, and all is mended:
   That you have but slumb'red here,
   While these visions did appear. (V.i. 422-425)   cupk **Puck**
   Play: a mdsumreim sihtgn aemrd **A MIDSUMMER NIGHT'S DREAM**

5. The more my wrong, the more his spite appears.
   What, did he marry me to famish me? (IV.iii. 2-3)   aekt **Kate**
   Play: eht giamtn fo eth wehrs   **THE TAMING OF THE SHREW**

Speakers: ghost, Skylock, Puck, Kate, Lear

Titles: A Midsummer Night's Dream, Anthony and Cleopatra, The Merchant of Venice, The Taming of the Shrew, Hamlet, Henry IV, King Lear, Romeo and Juliet, Othello

Page 36

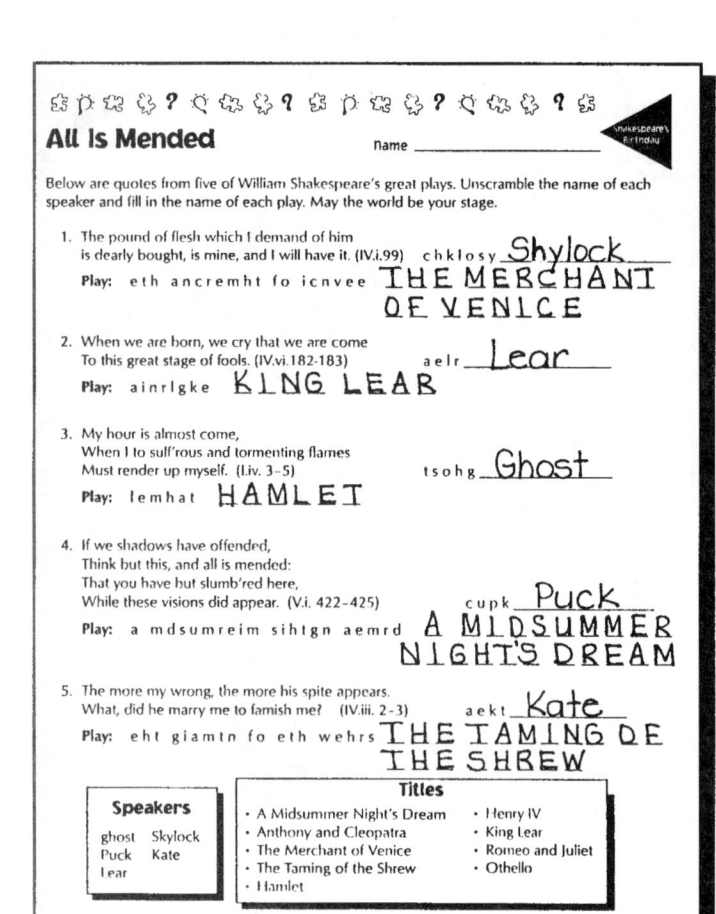

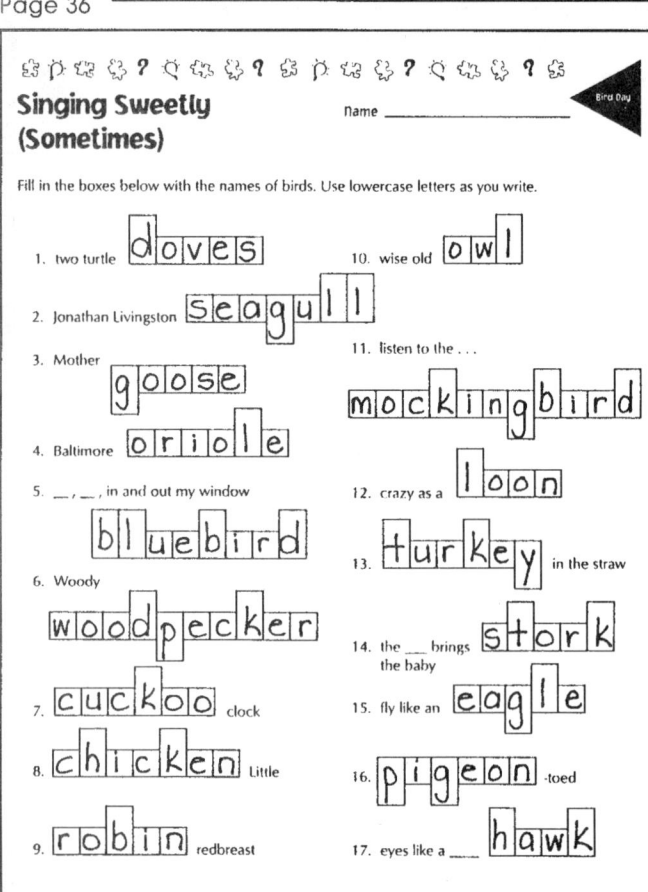

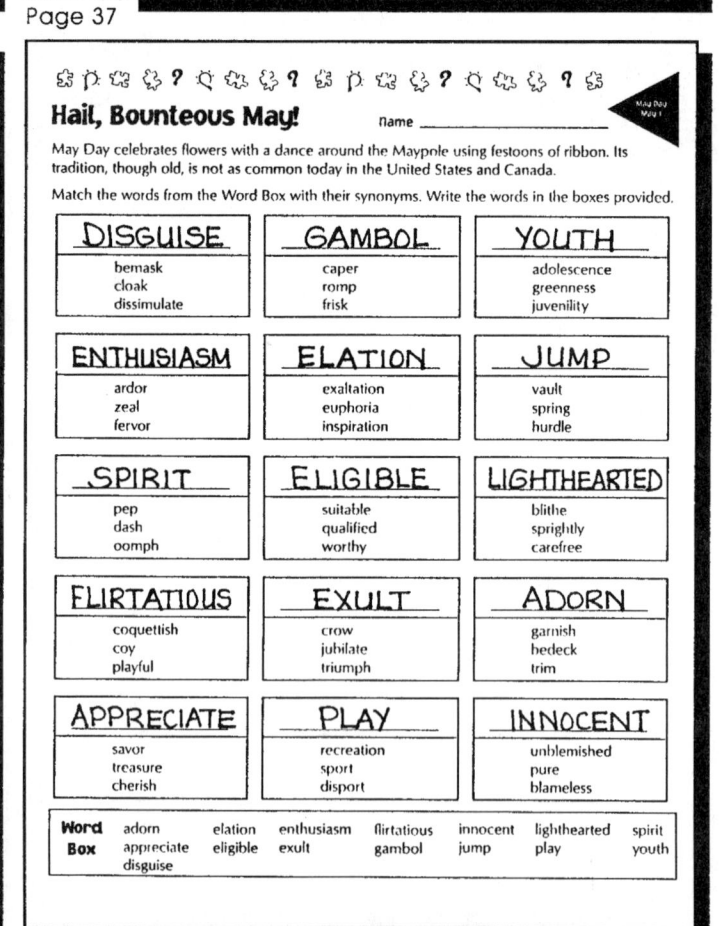

Bow to the Bard

Fit the letters of each column into the boxes directly above them to form words. The letters may or may not go into the boxes in the same order in which they are given. The finished puzzle will give the names of seven of William Shakespeare's plays.

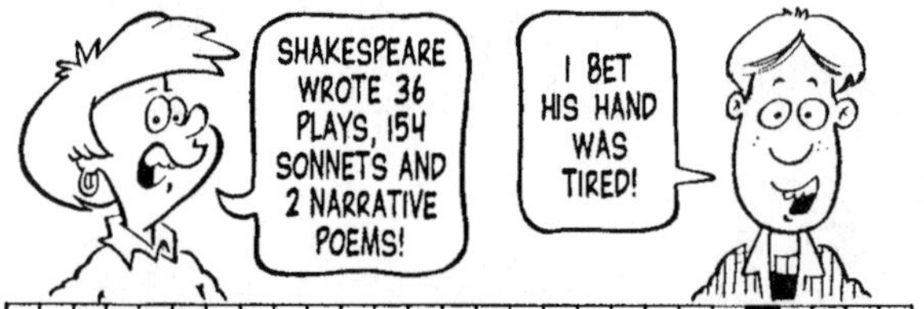

Speech bubble: SHAKESPEARE WROTE 36 PLAYS, 154 SONNETS AND 2 NARRATIVE POEMS!
Speech bubble: I BET HIS HAND WAS TIRED!

Filled grid:
THE*MERCHANT*OF*VENICE*OTHE
LLO*KING*LEAR*THE*TEMPEST*R
OMEO*AND*JULIET*A*MIDSUMMER
*NIGHTS*DREAM*JULIUS*CAESAR

Title List: Julius Caesar, Romeo and Juliet, The Tempest, Othello, King Lear, The Merchant of Venice, A Midsummer Nights Dream

Hint: Some words may wrap to a second line.

Page 37

Singing Sweetly (Sometimes)

Fill in the boxes below with the names of birds. Use lowercase letters as you write.

1. two turtle **doves**
2. Jonathan Livingston **seagull**
3. Mother **goose**
4. Baltimore **oriole**
5. _, _, in and out my window **bluebird**
6. Woody **woodpecker**
7. **cuckoo** clock
8. **chicken** Little
9. **robin** redbreast
10. wise old **owl**
11. listen to the... **mockingbird**
12. crazy as a **loon**
13. **turkey** in the straw
14. the ___ brings the baby **stork**
15. fly like an **eagle**
16. **pigeon**-toed
17. eyes like a **hawk**

Page 38

Hail, Bounteous May!

May Day celebrates flowers with a dance around the Maypole using festoons of ribbon. Its tradition, though old, is not as common today in the United States and Canada.

Match the words from the Word Box with their synonyms. Write the words in the boxes provided.

DISGUISE	**GAMBOL**	**YOUTH**
bemask	caper	adolescence
cloak	romp	greenness
dissimulate	frisk	juvenility

ENTHUSIASM	**ELATION**	**JUMP**
ardor	exaltation	vault
zeal	euphoria	spring
fervor	inspiration	hurdle

SPIRIT	**ELIGIBLE**	**LIGHTHEARTED**
pep	suitable	blithe
dash	qualified	sprightly
oomph	worthy	carefree

FLIRTATIOUS	**EXULT**	**ADORN**
coquettish	crow	garnish
coy	jubilate	hedeck
playful	triumph	trim

APPRECIATE	**PLAY**	**INNOCENT**
savor	recreation	unblemished
treasure	sport	pure
cherish	disport	blameless

Word Box: adorn, elation, enthusiasm, flirtatious, innocent, lighthearted, spirit, appreciate, eligible, exult, gambol, jump, play, youth, disguise

Page 39

Birthday for Buddha

Place the letters in each column in the boxes directly above them to form words. The letters may or may not go in the boxes in the same order in which they are given. Your finished puzzle will give part of the Buddha story.

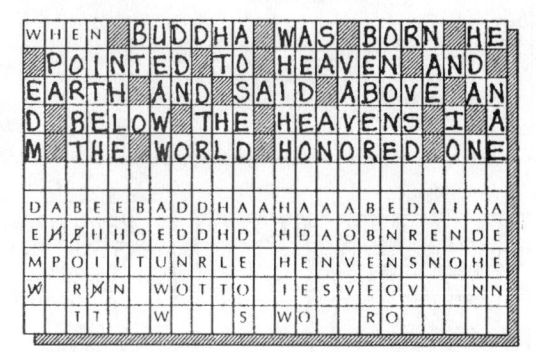

```
W H E N   B U D D H A   W A S   B O R N   H E
P O I N T E D   T O   H E A V E N   A N D
E A R T H   A N D   S A I D   A B O V E   A N
D   B E L O W   T H E   H E A V E N S   I   A
M   T H E   W O R L D   H O N O R E D   O N E
```

Buddha means enlightened one!

Hint: Some words may wrap to a second line.

Mom and Me

In honor of all mothers in the world, enjoy this poem by Ogden Nash entitled "The Guppy." Place the letters in each column in the boxes directly above them to form words. The letters may or may not go in the boxes in the same order in which they are given.

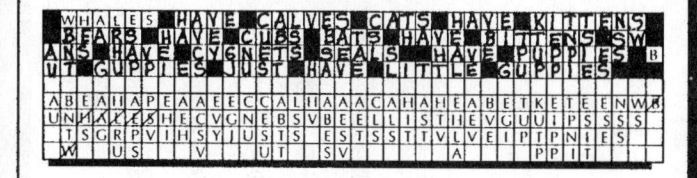

```
W H A L E S   H A V E   C A L V E S   C A T S   H A V E   K I T T E N S
B E A R S   H A V E   C U B S   B A T S   H A V E   B I T T E N S
S W A N S   H A V E   C Y G N E T S   S E A L S   H A V E   P U P P I E S
B U T   G U P P I E S   J U S T   H A V E   L I T T L E   G U P P I E S
```

Ogden Nash also collaborated on the 1943 musical "One Touch of Venus"...it was a big hit!

Hint: Some words may wrap to a second line.

Words Cannot Describe (but I'll try)

Fill in this chart using words that begin with the letters shown at the top of each column. Find as many as you can. You may use information sources to help your search. Have 2 or 3 others complete charts too. Then compare your answers crossing out any duplicates. See which person has the most items unmarked.

POSSIBILITIES INCLUDE

Category	A	D	O	R	E
Famous women (last names)	Jane Addams	Elizabeth Dole	Annie Oakley	Sally Ride	Amelia Earhart
Verbs that show a mother's actions	adore	discipline	organize	remind	educate
Occupations	author	dancer	organist	reporter	engineer
Flowers or trees your mother might give you	aster	dogwood	orchid	rose	elm

---

The Lady with the Lamp

May 12 is the birthdate of Florence Nightingale, a person important to hospital reforms of the 19th and 20th centuries. Use the clues to scramble and add one letter to each word to form a new word associated with the work and life of Florence Nightingale.

Letters to be added include: d d h l l m m n o o r r u y y

	Word	Letter	New Word	Hint
1.	those	O	SOOTHE	to calm, relieve, or pacify
2.	down	U	WOUND	an injury
3.	pal	M	LAMP	instrument of light
4.	saw	R	WARS	skirmishes where Nightingale aided
5.	dice	M	MEDIC	a physician
6.	places	L	SCALPEL	a cutting tool in surgery
7.	bold	O	BLOOD	life fluid
8.	vase	L	SALVE	a healing ointment
9.	sure	N	NURSE	one who cares for the sick
10.	ale	H	HEAL	to recover, to restore the body
11.	heat	D	DEATH	the sorrow of war
12.	scorers	D	RED CROSS	a world health agency
13.	licks	Y	SICKLEY	ill, unhealthy
14.	yam	R	ARMY	a military unit
15.	tail	Y	ITALY	Nightingale's birth country, like a boot

She was the first woman awarded the British Order of Merit!

We Salute You!

This holiday celebration was begun after the Civil War to honor those who died for our nation, both North and South.

Find the 5-letter words related to *Memorial Day* by the process of elimination and deduction. Fill in the blanks with five-letter answers to each definition. The number in parentheses tells how many of the letters in the answer are also in the Secret Word. The boxes tell you the correct position(s). The first one is done for you.

secret word — **H O N O R**

to burn with hot liquid	s	c	a	l	d	(2)
to experience with pleasure	e	n	j	o	y	(1)
aircraft *driver*	p	i	l	o	t	(1)
wails or cries like a baby	b	a	w	l	s	(0)
very hot vapor	s	t	e	a	m	(0)
stallion, for example	h	o	r	s	e	(3)
cocoa-colored, for example	b	r	o	w	n	(3)
listened	h	e	a	r	d	(2)
instruments for doing work	t	o	o	l	s	(2)

secret word — **G R A V E**

to expell	e	v	i	c	t	(2)
horizontal ledge	s	h	e	l	f	(1)
tongue of fire	f	l	a	m	e	(2)
deep, angry, dog noise	g	r	o	w	l	(2)
wooly, fluffy	f	u	z	z	y	(0)
hazy; unspecific	v	a	g	u	e	(4)
a small riot	b	r a	w	l	(2)
having much foliage	l	e	a	f	y	(2)
the entire amount, all	w	h	o	l	e	(1)

Page 44

We Remember

Find 31 words related to Memorial Day in this wordsearch.

Word Bank

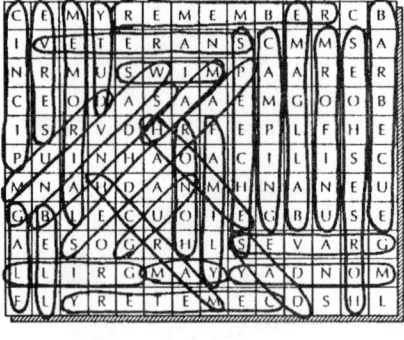

ballgame	duty	ham	memorial	serve
bands	family	home	Monday	speeches
barbecue	flag	honor	parades	swim
bell	grill	horseshoes	picnic	uniform
camping	graves	march	remember	veterans
cemetery	gun	May	sad	waving
drum				

MEMORIAL DAY WAS FIRST WIDELY OBSERVED ON MAY 30, 1868!

Extra: How many words can you create using the letters in these words?
flowers for soldiers

Page 45

The Picture-esque Americas

Figure out the names of these countries of the Americas. Each picture represents a letter of the alphabet. Note that some letters may be represented by more than one picture symbol.

1. P a n a m a
2. C h i l e
3. M e x i c o
4. B o l i v i a
5. C a n a d a
6. B e l i z e

Now design your own picture puzzles for these four countries:
Costa Rica   Argentina   Honduras   Brazil

Page 46

Wave Your Flag High

To complete this page rearrange the letters to form the name of a Canadian province or U.S. state. Your completed puzzle will share a slogan true to each country.

1. This state flag shows a red **C** overlaying two blue stripes and one white horizontal stripe.
   O COLD OAR
2. This state flag shows a white palm tree and a crescent moon on a blue background.
   AN OIL CRUSH OAT
3. This provincial flag shows a square-sailed vessel with four oars.
   WIN WRECK BUNS
4. This state flag shows a yellow torch surrounded by 19 stars on a blue background.
   AIDA INN
5. This provincial flag shows the Union Jack in the upper left corner and a buffalo on a red background.
   BOAT MAIN
6. This state flag shows a bear, a red star, and a red stripe on a white background.
   IF ACORN AIL
7. This state flag shows a ceremonial Indian shield on a blue background.
   LO HAM OAK
8. This state flag shows three red, three white, and two blue horizontal stripes with a Union Jack in the upper left corner.
   AW I AH I
9. This state flag has two red stripes criss-crossing its white field.
   A BAA ALM
10. This provincial flag shows 4 white *fleurs-de-lis* surrounding a white cross on a blue background.
    BE CUE Q
11. This state flag has a copper-colored star from which red and yellow rays extend. The bottom half of the flag is blue.
    AN OZ AIR
12. This state flag shows three white stars in a blue circle on a red field. One blue stripe runs down the right-hand edge.
    SEEN TEENS
13. This state flag shows a white buffalo in a blue field with a white and red border.
    MY NOWIG

1. COLORADO
2. SOUTHCAROLINA
3. NEWBRUNSWICK
4. INDIANA
5. MANITOBA
6. CALIFORNIA
7. OKLAHOMA
8. HAWAII
9. ALABAMA
10. QUEBEC
11. ARIZONA
12. TENNESSEE
13. WYOMING

Page 47

G'mornin', Poppa!

Fill in the blanks below with synonyms of the words in parentheses. Then use the suggested letter from the replacement word to find the answer to the riddle.

Word Bank

assistive	jaunt	sagacious
cherish	leggings	shrewd
dexterous	mindless	slumber
engaged	pacifistic	vintage
globoid	rightful	windy

1. G'morning, Poppa! Oh, did I wake you? I just wanna say how much I (appreciate) **cherish** (2nd letter) you. 2. There's that (distinctive) **vintage** (1st letter) furrow above your eyes that makes you look so smart. 3. Oh, by the way, I gotcha these (socks) **leggings** (5th letter). I hope they fit. If not, I guess I'll hafta wear them myself. 4. And I just want you to know I was wrong to smash in the headlight and your discipline was (just) **rightful** (2nd letter). 5. I promise to be more (helpful) **assistive** (6th letter) next time I change the lightbulb in the garage. 6. It's too bad you were so (busy) **engaged** (1st letter) retrieving the golf balls that I putted into the street. 7. Yeah, Poppa, you were definitely (wise) **sagacious** (3rd letter) to lock your golf clubs in your bedroom closet. 8. And I wanna say how (handy) **dexterous** (4th letter) you are putting in all those locks on the closets throughout the house. 9. Did you (sleep) **slumber** (4th letter) long enough last night? 10. I guess my music at two in the morning was a bit (thoughtless) **mindless** (6th letter) of me, huh? 11. Do you think I'm a bit too (talkative) **windy** (3rd letter) this morning? 12. Well, if you think so, you must be right. You're one (clever) **shrewd** (6th letter) dude. 13. Hey, what's that (round) **globoid** (3rd letter) object in your hand? 14. You're not plannin' to throw that baseball at me, are you? But you're so (nonviolent) **pacifistic** (6th letter)! 15. . . . You're sending me on a (trip) **jaunt** (2nd letter) to Aunt Mabel's in Cleveland. I'll miss you, Poppa!

Riddle: What should you remember for Father's Day?

D O N ' T   G I V E   H I M   A   T I E
12 13 11 5 7 4 2 10 1 14 9 15 8 3 6

Page 48

Warm and Sunny

Fill in the boxes with words for summer. Use lowercase letters as you write.

1. mound of a six-legged social crawler — **anthill**
2. America's pastime — **baseball**
3. cool cone or bowl dessert — **icecream**
4. "in the _____ ol' summertime" — **good**
5. refreshing water sport _____ — **skiing**
6. pesky blood-sucking insect — **mosquito**
7. family outing in tent — **camping**
8. large, red-pulped fruit from a vine — **watermelon**
9. invention that cools room — **air conditioner**
10. fruit with seeds on its "skin" — **strawberry**
11. beautifully colored day creature — **butterfly**
12. these protect the *blinkers* from old Sol — **sunglasses**
13. sweet or tart fruit of the season — **cherry**
14. bee's stinging cousin — **wasp**
15. hot day exercise — **swimming**

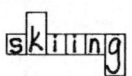

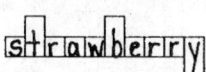

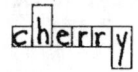

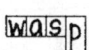

Page 49

A Simmerin' Summer

Annie and four friends celebrate the first day of summer in five different ways. Each begins his/her activities at a different time of the day. Use the matrix to find out what each one does and when each begins.

Clues:
1. Carrie, who didn't go on a picnic, isn't the girl who went to the pool at 10:30 A.M.
2. Ben began his activity at least two hours after the girl who mowed lawns.
3. Elsie, the one at the beach, and the 11:30 A.M. beginner are 3 different people.
4. The swimmer at the pool began after the mower but before the boy at the beach. None of these people began at 9:00 A.M.
5. Daryl is the dog walker.
6. The picnicker began after the one at the pool.

	mow grass	go to beach	swim in pool	walk dog	have picnic	9:00 A.M.	9:30 A.M.	10:30 A.M.	11:30 A.M.	1:00 P.M.
Annie					X				X	
Ben		X								X
Carrie	X						X			
Daryl				X		X				
Elsie			X					X		

SORRY DUDE...I'M NOT OUT OF BED UNTIL NOON!

Page 50

Overcoming Adversity

Use the code to complete the quotation about Helen Keller. Follow the code row by row until all the blanks are filled in. Cross off each letter square as you use it. The first word has been done for you.

Code: 5 2 7 3 6 8 1 4

HELEN KELLER GRADUATED WITH HONORS FROM RADCLIFFE COLLEGE IN 1904!

ALTHOUGH BLIND, DEAF, AND MUTE DUE TO A CHILDHOOD FEVER, HELEN KELLER BECAME A WORLD-RENOWNED AUTHOR AND SPEAKER. TODAY WE RECALL HER TEACHER, ANNE SULLIVAN, AS "THE MIRACLE WORKER".

Page 51

© Instructional Fair • TS Denison

IF8728 *Challenge Your Mind*

In Praise of Summer

Fit the letters in each column into the boxes directly above them to form words. The letters may or may not go into the boxes in the same order in which they are given. One word is done for you. Your finished puzzle may give you summer cheer. Enjoy your vacation!

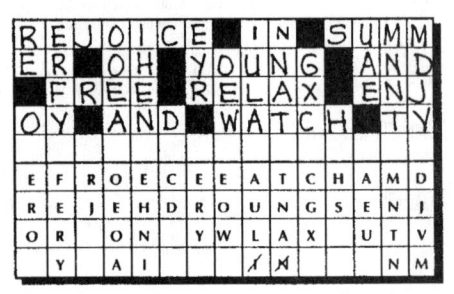

R	E	J	O	I	C	E		I	N		S	U	M	M
E	R		O	H		Y	O	U	N	G		A	N	D
	F	R	E	E		R	E	L	A	X		E	N	J
O	Y		A	N	D		W	A	T	C	H			T
														Y

E	F	R	O	E	C	E	E	A	T	C	H	A	M	D
R	E	J	E	H	D	R	O	U	N	G	S	E	N	J
O	R		O	N		Y	W	L	A	X		U	T	V
	Y		A	I										N M

Speech bubble: "I, LIKE, YOU KNOW REALLY DIG SUMMER!"

Hint: Some words may wrap to a second line.

Page 52

The Great North Country

Each entry is written in code. Use the clues to decode the mystery and name the terms.

Clue	Entry	Answer
1. Canada's capital city	DEERCR	OTTAWA
2. what this day honors, Canada's ___	QWLBVBWLBWZB	INDEPENDENCE
3. country which once "owned" Canada	PNBRE GNQERQW	GREAT BRITAIN
4. Canada's government leader	VNQKB KQWQUEBN	PRIME MINISTER
5. Canadian "state"	VNDSQWZB	PROVINCE
6. Canada is the world's largest country	UBZDWL	SECOND
7. because it's so wide, Canada has six ___	EQKB FDWBU	TIME ZONES
8. its northern border	RNZEQZ DZBRW	ARCTIC OCEAN
9. easternmost province	WBCYDJWLORWL	NEWFOUNDLAND
10. city with annual stampede	ZROPRNT	CALGARY
11. chief Pacific port	SRWZDJSBN	VANCOUVER
12. famous Atlantic fishing site	PNRWL GRWHU	GRAND BANKS
13. watery highway to the interior	UE ORCNBWZB UBRCRT	ST. LAWRENCE SEAWAY
14. Albertan National Park	ARUVBN	JASPER
15. symbol of Canada	KRVOB OBRY	MAPLE LEAF
16. smallest province	VNQWZB BLCRNL QUORWL	PRINCE EDWARD ISLAND

Canada's Motto: YNDK UBR ED UBR
FROM SEA TO SEA

Speech bubble: CANADA'S NAME IS THOUGHT TO BE DERIVED FROM THE IROQUOIS WORD FOR COMMUNITY —KANATA!

Page 53

You're a Grand Old Flag!

Fill in this chart using words that begin with the letters shown at the top of each column. Find as many as you can. You may use information sources to help your search. Have 2 or 3 others complete charts too. Then compare your answers, crossing out any that duplicate. See which person has the most items unmarked.

POSSIBILITIES INCLUDE

Category	F	L	A	G	S
American Patriots (First or Last Names)	Franklin Roosevelt	Meriwether Lewis	Abe Lincoln	George Washington	Sally Ride
Sports, Games, and Other Activities	Frisbee Football Fishing	Lawn tennis	Archery Acrobats Aerobics	Golfing	Swimming
Picnic Food	Fish	Lemonade	Apple Pie	Granola Bars	Salad
Vacation Spots	Fair	Lake	Alaska Aquarium	Grand Canyon	Seashore

Page 54

At the Bridge

On this date in 1837, Ralph Waldo Emerson dedicated a memorial near a bridge in Concord, Massachusetts.

Use the Word Box to help you fill in the diagram to learn what he said. The quotation will read from left to right and some words wrap to the next line. We have included letters for some of the words to assist you.

Speech bubble: RALPH WALDO EMERSON ATTENDED HARVARD COLLEGE FROM 1817 TO 1821!

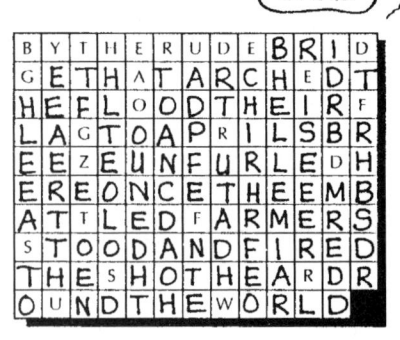

B	Y	T	H	E	R	U	D	E	B	R	I	D
G	E	T	H	A	T	A	R	C	H	E	D	T
H	E	F	L	O	O	D	T	H	E	I	R	F
L	A	G	T	O	A	P	R	I	L	S	B	R
E	E	Z	E	U	N	F	U	R	L	E	D	H
E	R	E	O	N	C	E	T	H	E	E	M	B
A	T	T	L	E	D	F	A	R	M	E	R	S
S	T	O	O	D	A	N	D	F	I	R	E	D
T	H	E	S	H	O	T	H	E	A	R	D	R
O	U	N	D	T	H	E	W	O	R	L	D	

Word Box

and	flood	the	bridge	round	world	stood
flag	the	breeze	once	unfurled	farmers	that
the	arched	here	to	embattled	shot	the
April's	heard	their	by	rude	fired	the

Page 55

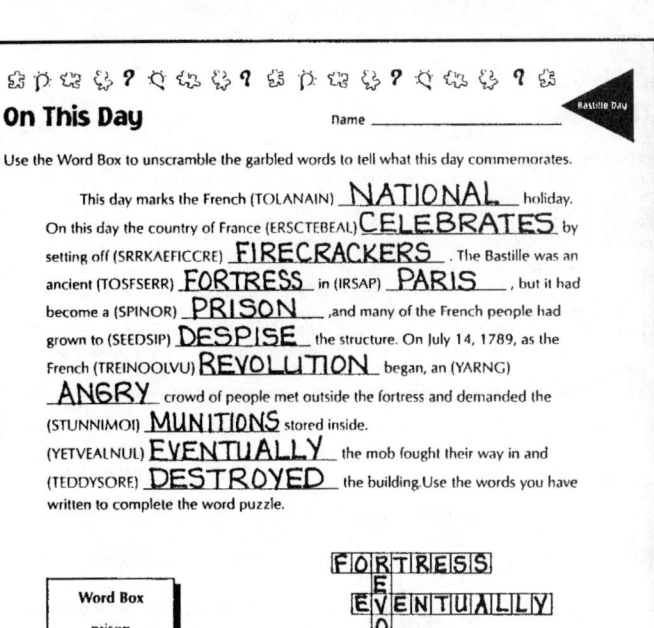

On This Day

Use the Word Box to unscramble the garbled words to tell what this day commemorates.

This day marks the French (TOLANAIN) **NATIONAL** holiday. On this day the country of France (ERSCTEBEAL) **CELEBRATES** by setting off (SRRKAEFICCRE) **FIRECRACKERS**. The Bastille was an ancient (TOSFSERR) **FORTRESS** in (IRSAP) **PARIS**, but it had become a (SPINOR) **PRISON**, and many of the French people had grown to (SEEDSIP) **DESPISE** the structure. On July 14, 1789, as the French (TREINOOLVU) **REVOLUTION** began, an (YARNG) **ANGRY** crowd of people met outside the fortress and demanded the (STUNNIMOI) **MUNITIONS** stored inside. (YETVEALNUL) **EVENTUALLY** the mob fought their way in and (TEDDYSORE) **DESTROYED** the building. Use the words you have written to complete the word puzzle.

Word Box: prison, eventually, national, despise, destroyed, fortress, angry, celebrates, Paris, munitions, revolution, firecrackers

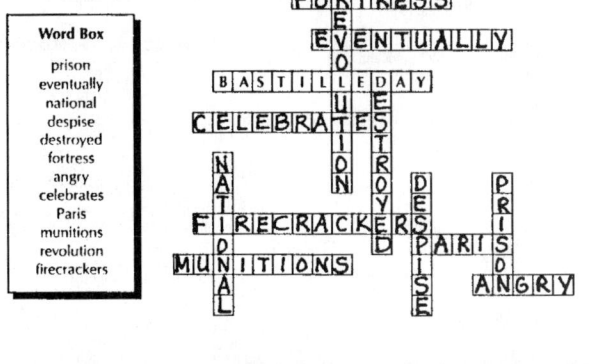

We All Scream for Ice Cream

Today is the day to enjoy this cool treat. Maybe you'll want to stay in the shade as you complete this word fill-in.

- **3 letters**: icy
- **4 letters**: bowl, cold, cone, foam, lick, soft
- **5 letters**: dairy, peach, split, swell, swirl, tasty
- **6 letters**: banana, frozen, malted, pecans, plenty, sundae, vanilla
- **7 letters**: chatter, tin roof
- **8 letters**: blue moon, snickers, Superman
- **9 letters**: bubblegum, pistachio, raspberry, rocky road, chocolate
- **10 letters**: strawberry
- **11 letters**: cookie dough, moosetracks
- **15 letters**: cookies and cream, cookies and fudge
- **16 letters**: marshmallow swirl, pralines and cream
- **17 letters**: mint chocolate chip
- **19 letters**: Mackinac Island fudge
- **20 letters**: strawberry cheesecake
- **21 letters**: chocolate peanutbutter

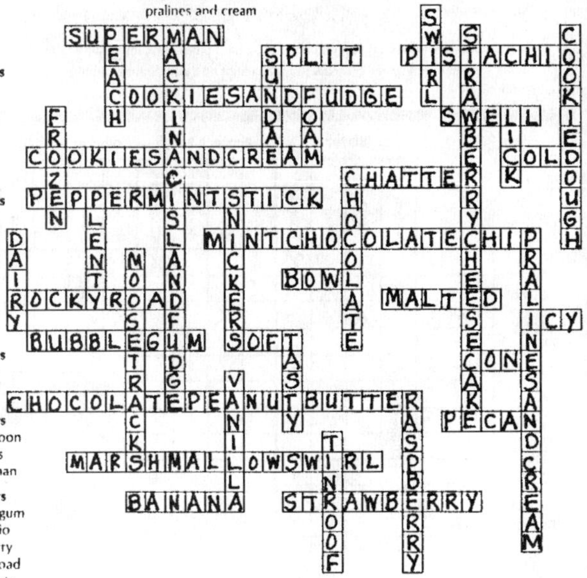

Lunar Madness

On this day in 1969, American astronauts first landed on the moon. In honor of that event try this puzzle about the moon and space. Each word or phrase below can be changed to a word or phrase relating to the space program. Use the definition clues whenever you become stuck. Good luck!

Words	Space Phrase	Definition Clue
1. TRACER (1 word)	CRATER	a pit in the moon's surface
2. CAPES (1 word)	SPACE	"the final frontier"
3. HEALTH DIES (2 words)	HEAT SHIELD	a protection against overheating upon re-entry
4. "LA LOOP" (1 word)	APOLLO	the craft type used in 1969
5. NASA TROUT (1 word)	ASTRONAUT	American space traveler
6. REMOTE (1 word)	METEOR	a shooting star
7. ARMS (1 word)	MARS	4th planet from the sun
8. DIET SOAR (1 word)	ASTEROID	"star shaped"
9. NEAR RIM (1 word)	MARINER	an early space satellite
10. THUS LET (1 word)	SHUTTLE	space taxi service
11. MINOR BOOST (2 words)	MOON'S ORBIT	lunar circle around us
12. GLANDULAR INN (2 words)	LUNAR LANDING	arrival on moon's surface
13. CLEFT NURSES (2 words)	REFLECTS SUN	how moon shines in night
14. ASK BITTY LOANS (2 words)	SKYLAB STATION	Earth's space platform
15. THE RAG VARSITY (2 words)	EARTH'S GRAVITY	what keeps us on Earth
16. MOTH MOAN NINE (4 words)	MAN-IN-THE-MOON	what some claim they see when they view our satellite

---

Beware the Flute Player!

Use the Word Box to write synonyms of the bold-faced words.

A visiting musician **came to** _entered_ Hamelin Town as its townsfolk **suffered** _endured_ an infestation of rats. The rats were causing a **horrid** _awful_ health hazard _danger_, that was killing many people. The numbers and fearlessness of these **marauding** _raiding_ rodents terrified the folk of Hamelin.

For whatever reason of his own, the town visitor **suggested** _proposed_ that he take responsibility for **driving** _propelling_ the vermin from the city. He asked an **exorbitant** _excessive_ fee to which the town council members gave false **pledge** _promise_ of payment. After he rid the town of its rats, playing his flute before the **packs** _swarms_, the pied-cloaked piper was denied **payment** _compensation_. We can well imagine his **seething** _boiling_ anger.

While records are slim in detail, we do know that the children of Hamelin vanished at **roughly** _about_ the same time as the unpaid piper. One **story** _tale_ claims that the children all suffered some **mysterious** _puzzling_ malady. The music-making flautist led the **wan** _pale_ children from the city while their parents prayed in the town's church. Were the children sold as slaves? Did they all **die** _succumb_ in the forest? We can only **guess** _surmise_. Yet a stained-glass window in the ancient Hamelin church **shows** _depicts_ a pied-cloaked piper, a rat, and a **child** _youngster_.

Word Box: about, awful, boiling, compensation, danger, depicts, endured, entered, excessive, pale, promise, proposed, propelling, puzzling, raiding, surmise, succumb, swarms, tale, youngster

---

© Instructional Fair • TS Denison — IF8728 Challenge Your Mind

Brother and Sister

This Hindu holiday honors brothers and sisters. Girls and women tie bracelets around the arms of their brothers who, in turn, promise to care for them. Use the clues below to match each brother and sister, identifying the color of each one's bracelet and the protection promised by each brother.

Clues:
1. Kacia, whose brother is not Lal, gave a blue bracelet. Zail did not receive this blue bracelet.
2. The brother who promised to protect his sister from dogs (not Kim) received a green bracelet.
3. Kim, who either received a gold or a red bracelet, promised to protect his sister from strangers.
4. Leema, who is promised protection from bullies, has no brother named Kim or Zail.
5. Indira's brother has a green bracelet. Shanda did not tie a gold bracelet around her brother's arm.

HINDUISM IS THE MAJOR RELIGION OF INDIA!

The Flash

On this day in 1945, the United States unleashed the atomic bomb on the city of Hiroshima. The immediate and following chaos shocked both the Japanese and the Allied nations. Nine days later the Japanese surrendered.

Match a word from the Word Box to its definition. The letter boxes may help you do this more easily.

Word Box

Atomic Bomb Dome, Hirohito, mushroom, Oppenheimer, Enola Gay, Honshu, Nagasaki, Ota River, fallout, Japan, nuclear weapon, Peace Memorial Park, genocide, Manahattan Project, O-Bon Festival, radiation sickness

1. a day to honor one's ancestors — **ObonFestival**
2. the plan for developing a nuclear weapon — **ManhattanProject**
3. the physicist who contributed most to develop the atomic bomb — **Oppenheimer**
4. seven tributaries feed this waterway at Hiroshima — **OtaRiver**
5. the shape of the after-flash cloud — **mushroom**
6. the emperor of Japan in 1945 — **Hirohito**
7. the B-29 which dropped the atomic bomb — **EnolaGay**
8. the descent of tiny particles of radioactive material — **fallout**
9. the ruins of the former Industrial Exhibition Hall — **AtomicBombDome**
10. symptoms of this were vomiting, internal bleeding, hair loss, and fever — **radiation sickness**

Panning in the Wild

Fill in the blanks with words from the Word Bank.

Word Bank: apart, book, Canada, crazy, enthusiast, gold, magic, many, million, more, mule, news, prospectors, remains, removed, rich, rushed, Skagway, territory, travel

When gold was found at Rabbit Creek in the Yukon **territory** of **Canada** in 1896, the **news** of its discovery spread quickly. By the following season folks were **crazy** with excitement. Adventurers from the world over **rushed** to the mining fields. One such **enthusiast** was Jack London who wrote about this **gold** rush life in his **book** White Fang.

More than 30,000 people dashed for the gold. Many of these would-be **rich** came by way of **Skagway** or Valdez in Alaska because of their proximitiy to the Klondike region. **Travel** to the fields was made possible by ship, raft, **mule**, dogsled, and foot. **Prospectors**, merchants, and thieves streamed in. Towns grew up like **magic** in a very short time.

The gold strike fell **apart** in 1910 and **many** of the prospectors and merchants left. But over 100 **million** dollars in ore had been **removed**. The town of Dawson, important then, **remains** the major town in the Klondike today.

Well, Blow Me Down!

On this day in 1851, the first America's Cup was held. The U.S. became most interested in this "sport of the sea." In each set, can you change the first word into the last word by changing one letter at a time to match the definitions?

Set 1
SAIL — 1st
MAIL — to send by post
MALL — a shopping center with many stores
MALE — opposite of a female
MACE — an evil weapon
RACE — last

Set 2
WIND — 1st
WAND — a magician's rod
WANE — to grow faint
WAVE — last

Set 3
SEA — 1st
PEA — a round green-pod veggie
PEP — spunk
PUP — a young seal
CUP — last

Set 4
MAST — 1st
MALT — like a chocolate shake
HALT — to stop
HALL — a corridor
HULL — last

Set 5
YAWL — 1st
BAWL — to wail
BALL — spherical toy
BALK — to stop short
BACK — behind
SACK — to fire (slang)
SOCK — argyle
DOCK — last

THE U.S. HELD THE AMERICA'S CUP FROM 1851 TO 1980!

Being Equal

Can you imagine a time when only men could vote? Until 1920, this was the practice in the United States. To read a quote from the 19th Amendment to the U.S. Constitution, fill in the blanks with letters from the chart in the order the code requires. Fill in letters from the first rows first, then move down until all letters are used. The first row has been started for you.

Code: 11-4-2-6-9-1-7-5-10-3-8

1	2	3	4	5	6	7	8	9	10	11
U	E	I	R	H	G	C	O	Y	T	T
N	I	T	T	O	Z	S	H	E	F	I
E	N	A	U	S	I	D	T	T	T	E
O	T	H	S	E	O	T	A	V	S	E
B	N	N	I	D	O	E	I	T	E	L
B	O	G	D	I	R	R	E	A	D	E
L	Y	T	B	N	T	U	E	H	I	D
F	T	B	S	O	A	S	Y	I	R	D
A	Y	N	N	E	S	T	A	T	O	A
I	O	E	C	F	U	O	X	N	S	C

NEW ZEALAND GAVE WOMEN THE RIGHT TO VOTE IN 1893!

THE RIGHT of citizens of the United States to vote shall not be denied or abridged by the United States or by any state on account of sex.

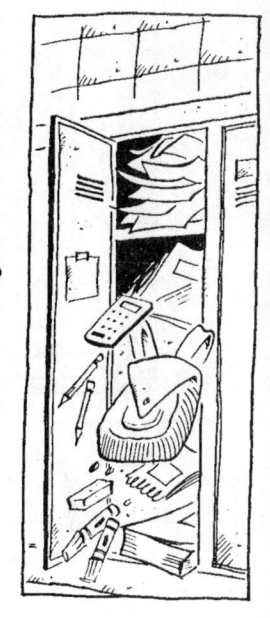

Page 64

Farewell, Summer!

Bumbling Bob is ready for school with the purchase of twenty items. His list is a bit disorganized. Unscramble the words to figure out what he bought.

1. CEILNPS — PENCILS
2. AEENOPPRT — NOTEPAPER
3. AEERRS — ERASER
4. CEHLMNNOUY — LUNCH MONEY
5. EEFILNPPTT — FELT TIP PEN
6. AEHIRSSTTW — SWEATSHIRT
7. DEFLORS — FOLDERS
8. EEHKOSSUY — HOUSE KEYS
9. CEGHLMOSTY — GYM CLOTHES
10. AACCLLORTU — CALCULATOR
11. AABCCKKP — BACKPACK
12. AEKMRRS — MARKERS
13. CEGGHIMNUW — CHEWING GUM
14. AEEJNNSW — NEW JEANS
15. BEKNOOOST — NOTEBOOKS
16. AACDFNOOS — CAN OF SODA

Page 65

Career Caper

On this day which honors workers in Canada and the United States, most people don't have to work! Is that strange, or what? Unscramble the words to list some of the possible occupations just waiting for you.

1. TTSIRA — A**RTIS**T
2. LTIIAIOPCN — P**OLITICIA**N
3. YTAOCRF RRWKOE — F**ACTORY WORKE**R
4. CRRSEEHEA — R**ESEARCHE**R
5. RLECK — C**LER**K
6. SREETFRO — F**ORESTE**R
7. TREIRW — W**RITE**R
8. TRAUOCDE — E**DUCATO**R
9. MARREF — F**ARME**R
10. MEALSSAN — S**ALESMA**N
11. NIECISTTS — S**CIENTIS**T
12. SEURN — N**URS**E
13. IENMR — M**INE**R
14. YNAIIHSPC — P**HYSICIA**N
15. TEALHET — A**THLET**E
16. DBIRUEL — B**UILDE**R
17. NAIINCEHTC — T**ECHNICIA**N
18. RATILO — T**AILO**R
19. RANUITJOLS — J**OURNALIS**T
20. TTEEERRINNA — E**NTERTAINE**R
21. LOCSAI RKOREW — S**OCIAL WORKE**R

MAYBE YOU COULD RAISE A HERD OF NAUGAS FOR LIKE, Y'KNOW... NAUGAHYDE!

Page 66

Your Not-So-Distant Past

Fill in the blanks and identify the words below. Then use the clues from the completed words to complete the phrase at the bottom of the page.

1. given to reverie; visionary — DREAMY (22 39 7 40 34 9)
2. six-sided polygons — HEXAGONS (2 28 6 35 38 44 18 25)
3. an eating utensil — FORK (11 32 8 46)
4. silly — FOOLISH (43 30 14 45 17 23 27)
5. spirit — SPUNK (48 13 5 36 20)
6. coarse — GRITTY (19 15 26 1 31)
7. fairly, rightfully — JUSTLY (29 47 24 16 37)
8. something carried; a burden — LOAD (4 10 40 22)
9. discoveries — FINDINGS (33 21 18 42 24 41 19 12)

HUH?

Phrase:

THE LUXURY OF SPOILING KIDS IS THE JOY OF MANY GRANDFOLKS

Page 67

See You Real Soon

It's the birthday of the most famous animated character of all time. Find 33 words related to Disney in the wordsearch including Mickey's names in French (Michel), Japanese (Miki), Spanish (Miguel), and Danish (Mikkel).

IS THIS PAGE A LITTLE GOOFY OR IS IT ME?

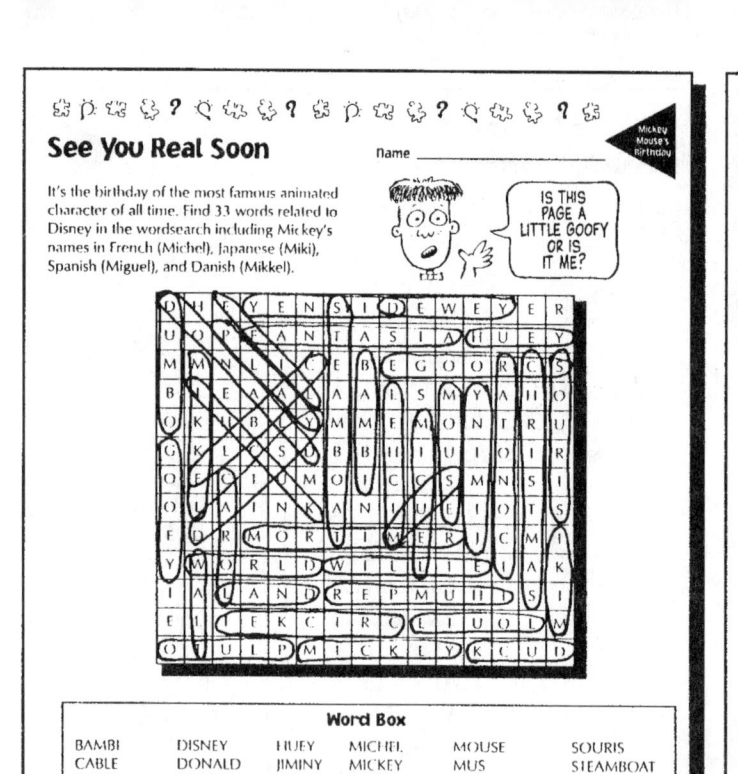

Word Box

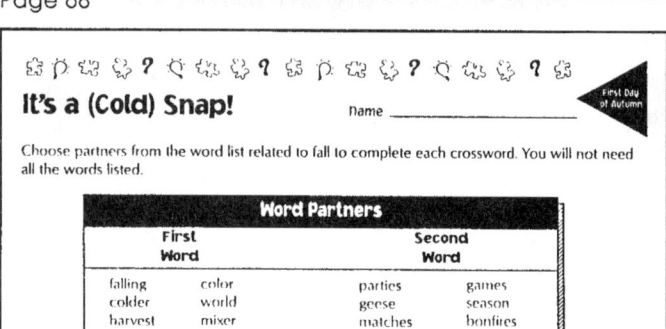

BAMBI	DISNEY	HUEY	MICHEL	MOUSE	SOURIS
CABLE	DONALD	JIMINY	MICKEY	MUS	STEAMBOAT
CAROL	DUCK	KUCHI	MIGUEL	PLAY	THUMPER
CHRISTMAS	DUMBO	LAND	MIKI	PLUTO	WALT
CRICKET	FANTASIA	LIFE	MIKKEL	RATONCITO	WILLIE
DAISY	GOOFY	LOUIE	MORTIMER	SCROOGE	WORLD
DEWEY					

What do the eleven remaining letters spell? **HERE'S MINNIE**

Page 68

Mr. Postman, Look and See

Write the words under the appropriate category.

Word Bank

selling stamps, announcements, next-day-delivery, care package, greeting card, parcel post, transporting, delivering, filing, first class, gifts, carrying, invitation, envelope, letter, mailbox, postcards, certified, photos, postage, pouch, priority, airmail, sorting, stamping, stamps, string, tape, C.O.D., third class, uniform, weighing

Jobs	Tools of Mailing	What Is Sent	How Sent
sorting	stamps	postcards	first class
delivering	postage	care package	certified
stamping	pouch	letters	C.O.D.
weighing	uniform	announcements	third class
transporting	tape	greeting cards	air mail
filing	string	invitations	priority
carrying	mailbox	photos	parcel post
selling stamps	envelope	gifts	next-day delivery

Here are some things you can do for the postal services:
1. Keep your pet restrained.
2. Write your address neatly on the envelope.
3. Keep a clear passage to your mailbox.
4. Say hello and smile at your carrier.
5. Send a thank you card to your service office.

YOU COULD REMEMBER TO PUT A STAMP ON THAT LETTER!

Page 69

It's a (Cold) Snap!

Choose partners from the word list related to fall to complete each crossword. You will not need all the words listed.

Word Partners

First Word		Second Word	
falling	color	parties	games
colder	world	geese	season
harvest	mixer	matches	bonfires
frosty	picking	leaves	flowers
football	racking	nights	yard
marching	drying	pumpkins	apples
caramel	making	series	temperature
glorious	sweater	bands	time
soccer	honking	tours	colors

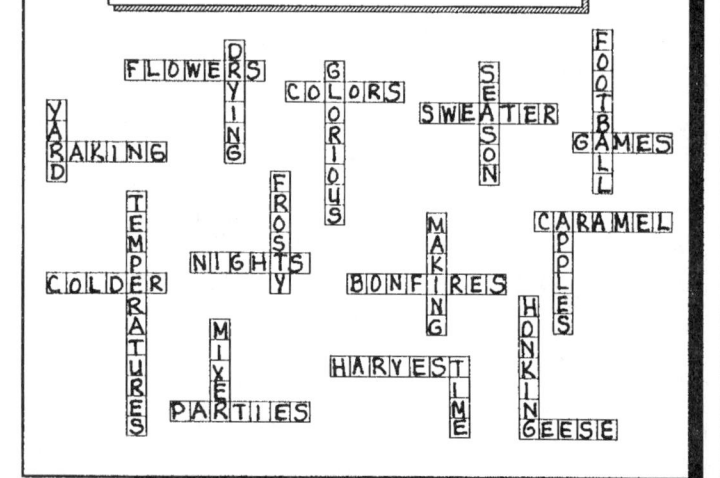

Crossword answers: FLOWERS, DRYING, COLORS, SEASON, SWEATER, FOOTBALL, YARD, RAKING, GLORIOUS, GAMES, TEMPERATURES, FROSTY, MAKING, CARAMEL, COLDER, NIGHTS, BONFIRES, APPLES, MIXED, HONKING, HARVEST, TIME, PARTIES, GEESE

Page 70

Grant Us Peace

Provide a word from the Word Box to match each meaning. Then use clues from the completed answers to build a phrase honoring peace. Words in the phrase may wrap to a second line.

a. a partial payment — DEPOSIT
b. haughty — ARROGANT
c. of subordinate importance — MINOR
d. to cry — WEEP
e. rebellions — COUPS
f. a style of cooking — CUISINE
g. to fling — HURL
h. an injury — WOUND
i. fit and hale — HEALTHY
j. to disable — CRIPPLE
k. very dirty — FILTHY
l. to comprehend — UNDERSTAND
m. wearliess — TIRELESS
n. a first-class aviator — ACE
o. an entrance — DOOR
p. to listen — HEAR
q. a strap for walking a dog — LEASH
r. a paddle — OAR
s. anxious — WORRIED
t. game item — CARD

Word Box

understand, cuisine, hear, filthy, healthy, cripple, coups, ace, weep, leash, oar, minor, tireless, door, worried, wound, deposit, hurl, arrogant, card

THE ENTIRE WORLD CRIES FOR PEACE MAY OUR WORLD LEADERS HEAR OUR CALL AND SILENCE THE GUNS WHICH POUND OUR SPIRITS INTO APATHY OR DESPAIR

Page 71

Grapple with Apples

What a wonderful day to think about apples! For each set, change the first word into the last *apple-inspired* word by changing one letter at a time to match the definitions.

Set 1
fan	1st word
PAN	baking platter
PIN	sharp fastener
PIE	tasty dessert

Set 2
bolts	1st word
BELTS	these hold up pants
BELLS	chimes
BELLY	tummy
JELLY	bread spread

Set 3
chap	1st word
CHIP	a crunchy potato
CHIN	under the mouth
THIN	lean
TWIN	one's clone
TWIG	from which an apple hangs

Set 4
place	1st word
PLATE	shallow dish
SLATE	type of rock
SPATE	a sudden flood
SPITE	malice
SMITE	to inflict a blow
SMITH	Granny's apple

Set 5
pit	1st word
LIT	set on fire
LID	cover
LAD	boy
DAD	his pa
DAY	opposite of night
SAY	speak
SPY	a sneaky apple variety

WOULD AN APPLE A DAY KEEP THIS PROBLEM AWAY?

Page 72

A Season to Praise

During the festival of Sukkoth, sometimes called the Feast of Tabernacles, the people build shelters called *sukkah*, which are covered with greens and decorated with harvest foods. Traditionally the holiday is a memorial to the time the Israelites wandered in the desert after they left Egypt. Each word defined below will fit alphabetically between the two words shown. The number of letters matches the blanks provided.

SUKKOTH IS ONE OF THE THREE JOYOUS PILGRIM FESTIVALS OF JUDAISM!

#				
1.	bugle	BUILD	bulb	to construct
2.	Custer	CUSTOM	cut	a tradition
3.	bottom	BOUGH	boulder	a branch or limb
4.	hart	HARVEST	has-been	to gather the crop
5.	booted	BOOTH	bootleg	a covered or enclosed stand
6.	automatic	AUTUMN	auxiliary	season before winter
7.	willing	WILLOW	willpower	the weeping tree
8.	reject	REJOICE	rejoin	to express gladness
9.	remedial	REMIND	remiss	to prod into remembering
10.	pallor	PALM	palooka	the tropical tree with dates

Page 73

A Hot Time in the Old Town Tonight

Firefighters of North America are among the best in the world. Their work in our communities is vital to the safety of all. Take time to thank them this week.

Match the words from List #2 to their antonyms in List #1. Write the appropriate letters on the lines in front of each number. Not all words from list 2 will be used. Remember that antonyms are words that mean the opposite.

List 1
Q 1. alarming
D 2. emergency
P 3. help
B 4. protected
O 5. rescue
K 6. adverse
R 7. friend
E 8. respond
L 9. safety
N 10. order
G 11. healthy
J 12. rush
A 13. heat
C 14. clean
H 16. vigorous

List 2
a. chill
b. unguarded
c. dirty
d. ordinariness
e. plan
f. ignore
g. ailing
h. lethargic
i. crew
j. meander
k. favorable
l. recklessness
m. calm
n. chaos
o. endanger
p. hinder
q. soothing
r. opponent
s. radio

AWW... SHUCKS!

Page 74

Charting the Explorers

Fill in this chart using words that begin with the letters shown at the top of each column. Find as many as you can. You may use information sources to help you search. Have 2 or 3 others complete charts too. Then compare your answers, crossing out any duplicates. See which person has the most squares marked.

POSSIBILITIES INCLUDE

	S	H	I	P	S
Transportation	Santa Maria	Horse	Ice boat	Pinta	Space Shuttle
Native American Tribes/Families	Sioux	Hopi	Inca	Potawatomi	Shoshoni
Verbs Related to Exploration	Scout	Hunt	Inquire	Plan	Search
Languages of the World	Swahili	Hebrew	Italian	Polish	Spanish
Occupations from the 15-16th Centuries	Silversmith	Herdsman	Inkmaker	Peasant	Sailor

Page 75

© Instructional Fair • TS Denison

IF8728 Challenge Your Mind

Explor-a-tion

Add letter groups to each of these -tion endings to find words which fit the phrases below.

Letter Groups

an	da	fas	hi	la	na	per	pre	ra	sti	ta	ti	vi
ci	ex	frus	in	mi	pa	plo	ra	sen	su	ter	tra	vi
ci	ex	ga	in	na	pa	pre	ra	si	ta	ti	ven	

1. In order to get funding for his voyage, Columbus had to make a _____ — PRESENTAtion
2. Columbus' hope for reaching the Far East filled him with _____ — ANTICIPAtion
3. Upon reaching land, Columbus might very well have experienced overwhelming _____ — EXHILARAtion
4. When Columbus reached the New World, he spent much time in _____ — EXPLORAtion
5. When his officers quarreled, Columbus may have been required to use _____ — INTERVENtion
6. To sail the seas, Columbus had to possess skills of _____ — NAVIGAtion
7. Columbus' love of maps bordered on this _____ — FASCINAtion
8. Organizing for the voyages undoubtedly meant much _____ — PREPARAtion
9. The native people may have hoped the Europeans' first _____ would be their last — VISITAtion
10. When they could not easily persuade native people to help them, the Europeans sometimes resorted to _____ — INTIMIDAtion
11. Because Columbus never reached China, he may have experienced _____ — FRUSTRAtion
12. _____ led some explorers to fear sea monsters and singing sea maids — SUPERSTItion

Page 76

Papa Wordsmith

On this day in 1758, Mr. Noah Webster was born. We remember him for his labor with an American-English Dictionary. Decode the symbols below to find these Webster-minded words.

1. ALLITERATION
2. FORESHADOW
3. LINGUISTICS
4. SYNTAX
5. VERBOSE
6. DIALECT
7. ETYMOLOGY
8. OXYMORON
9. EUPHEMISM
10. TERMINOLOGY
11. PUN
12. ACCENT
13. ORATORY
14. LEXICOGRAPHIC

Locate five of these words in the dictionary and write their meanings on the back of this sheet.

Page 77

We Are the World

This august council of world representatives, the United Nations, is more than fifty years old. Unscramble the puzzled words to learn more.

1. The United Nations was established in (NETINENE YRTFO EFIV) Nineteen forty five.
2. The U.N. began with (IFYTF - NEO) fifty-one -member countries.
3. Three main goals of the U.N. are to:
   a. maintain international (ACEEP) peace
   b. promote (AELQU ITGRHS) equal rights,
   c. and achieve (ACEEIOOPRTV) cooperative solutions to world problems.
4. The six main bodies of the U.N. are:
   a. the General (ABFLMSSY) Assembly,
   b. the (CEIRSTUY LOINUCC) Security Council,
   c. the (CCEIMNOO) Economic and Social Council,
   d. the (EEHIPRSSTTU) Trusteeship Council,
   e. the (AACEEIRRSTT) Secretariat,
   f. and the International (CORTU) Court of Justice.
5. The Security Council has 15 representative countries of which five are permanent members. These five are:
   a. (ACHIN) China
   b. (ACEFNR) France
   c. (AIRSSU) Russia
   d. (DEINTU AESSTT) United States
   e. (DEINTU DIGKMNO) United Kingdom
6. The six official languages of the U.N. are:
   a. (AABCIR) Arabic
   b. (CEEHINS) Chinese
   c. (EGHILNS) English
   d. (CERHNF) French
   e. (AINRSSU) Russian
   f. (AHINPSS) Spanish

Page 78

Know Your World

Unscramble the names of twenty countries of our world. Some are near and some are distant. The continent where each country can be found has been given as a clue.

		Country	Continents
1.	ADEILNRSTWZ	Switzerland	Europe
2.	AEIRZ	Kenya	Africa
3.	AEEGLNS	Senegal	Africa
4.	AGRUUUY	Uruguay	South America
5.	ABINOS	Bosnia	Europe
6.	OLVBIAI	Bolivia	South America
7.	AIRSY	Syria	Asia
8.	CCMOOOR	Morocco	Africa
9.	LAZRIB	Brazil	South America
10.	AAAACDGMRS	Madagascar	Africa
11.	ADEIINNOS	Indonesia	Asia
12.	AABCDIMO	Cambodia	Asia
13.	AGLOPRTU	Portugal	Europe
14.	ACDEILN	Iceland	Europe
15.	AAACDN	Canada	North America
16.	BEGILMU	Belgium	Europe
17.	AEINOST	Estonia	Europe
18.	AAGNUY	Guyana	South America

Page 79

© Instructional Fair • TS Denison

IF8728 Challenge Your Mind

Things That Go Bump

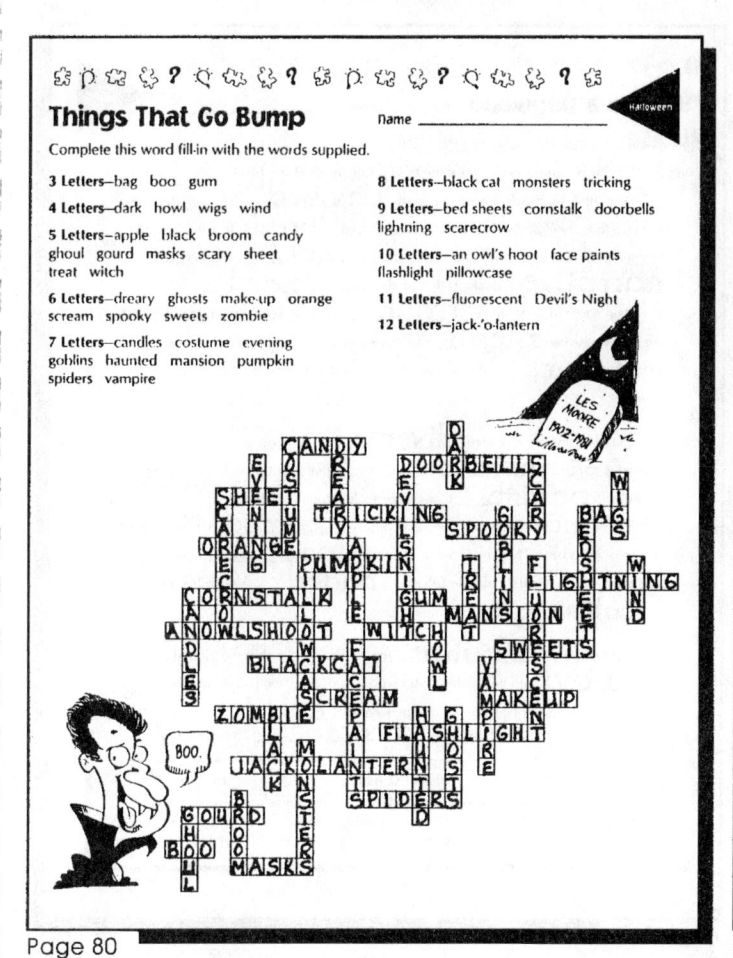

Complete this word fill-in with the words supplied.

3 Letters—bag boo gum
4 Letters—dark howl wigs wind
5 Letters—apple black broom candy ghoul gourd masks scary sheet treat witch
6 Letters—dreary ghosts make-up orange scream spooky sweets zombie
7 Letters—candles costume evening goblins haunted mansion pumpkin spiders vampire
8 Letters—black cat monsters tricking
9 Letters—bed sheets cornstalk doorbells lightning scarecrow
10 Letters—an owl's hoot face paints flashlight pillowcase
11 Letters—fluorescent Devil's Night
12 Letters—jack-'o-lantern

Page 80

A Frightful Custom

Fit the Word Box words sensibly into the sentences.

The Celtic **festival** of Samhain marked the last day of the Celtic **year**. These early Celts believed that the **spirits** of the dead **returned** on this evening. Food and **lights** were placed outside houses so these **ghosts** would feel at home.

In later times, people who went **outdoors** after dark would wear **costumes** so witches and other evil spirits would not recognize them. In some villages, the townsfolk would go house to house begging for food for their **community** feasts. Those who **willingly** and big heartedly gave food would be guaranteed a **prosperous** new year.

According to Irish legend, a most **evil** man named Jack tricked the devil. Because he was not fit for heaven and because the **devil** would not accept him, this Jack, upon death, was forced to walk about Earth **carrying** a gourd, a jack-o'-lantern.

Halloween became **popular** in the U.S. and Canada as Irish families immigrated into these **countries** in the 1800s.

Harry Houdini, the eminent **escape** artist, died while **performing** on this day in 1926.

Word Box
carrying
prosperous
spirits
festival
year
devil
performing
popular
escape
ghosts
community
lights
evil
willingly
returned
countries
outdoors
costumes

Page 81

Hindu Festival of Lights

LAKSHMI IS ALSO THE WIFE OF HINDU GOD VISHNU!

Diwali is the holiday of India that signifies the end of harvest and the beginning of winter. During this festival **Lakshmi**, the Hindu goddess of good luck and prosperity, comes to people's homes and is greeted by lamps called *dipa*.

Fit the letters in each column into the boxes directly above them to form words. The letters may or may not go into the boxes in the same order in which they are given. Some words may wrap to the next line. Your finished puzzle is a plea to this goddess.

COME INTO OUR HOME LAKSHIMA
WE WAIT FOR YOUR PRESENCE FO
R YOU ARE THE GODDESS OF WEA
LTH AND WE WISH TO HONOR YOU

Word Box
Goddess	wealth	are	your	into	presence
you (2)	honor	wait	wish	honor	the
home	Lakshima	and	of	our	to
come		for (2)	we (2)		

Page 82

Add or Subtract

When the early Christian church set aside a day to honor the many saints killed for their faith, they chose the day of Samhaim, a feared day which recalled spirits of the dead and evil beings. In this activity, add to, or subtract letters from the words listed to form a word or phrase associated with these two holidays.

Letter Bank A C E E F I M M O R R T T U X

1. stolen key	-y	skeleton	structural body organ
2. sane trap	-r	peasant	serf
3. frame	-m	fear	dread
4. cards	+e	sacred	holy
5. pang	+a	pagan	heathen
6. rustiest point	-t	superstition	belief in omens
7. trial	+u	ritual	rite
8. mend	+o	demon	devil
9. thread	-r	death	demise
10. meal	+f	flame	fire
11. whit	+c	witch	sorceress
12. sat gave	-t	savage	wild
13. tarry	+m	martyr	life sacrificer
14. trips	+i	spirit	ghost

Page 83

© Instructional Fair • TS Denison

IF8728 *Challenge Your Mind*

Writer's Niche

Fill in this chart using words that begin with the letters shown at the side of each column. The columns are independent of one another. In other words, you don't have to list a work written by the author you list. Find as many as you can. You may use information sources to help your search. Have 2 or 3 others complete charts too. Then compare your answers, crossing out any duplicates. See which person has the most squares unmarked?

POSSIBILITIES INCLUDE

	Last Names of Famous Authors	Writers' Tools	Types of Writing	Writers' Actions	Works of Famous Fiction
W	Wright	wide-ruled paper	wise sayings	write	Wolves of Willoughby Chase
R	Rogers	ribbon	report	rhyme	Rabbit Hill
I	Innocenti	ink	introspective	inform	Island of the Blue Dolphins
T	Taylor	typewriter	theme	type	Tuck Everlasting
E	Enright	encyclopedia	exposition	entertain	Exodus
R	Robinson	resource book	riddle	revise	Runaway Ralph

Page 84

I'll Have a Dagwood, Please

Using the Word Box, write synonyms for the bold-faced words in the blanks.

We think sandwiches were **invented** _devised_ by John Montagu, the Fourth Earl of Sandwich, who was so **attracted** _lured_ to gambling that he refused to leave his card table to grab a **bite** _meal_. The **account** _narrative_ declares that he **dispatched** _sent_ his servant to obtain some meat to **place** _stick_ between two slices of bread. When the other **patrons** _clients_ saw the order which the returning servant **carried** _bore_, they did not forget. Sandwiches have been with us ever since.

Sandwiches are as **varied** _diverse_ as humans. Sandwiches may be **made** _assembled_ from bagels, croissants, and pita bread. They may be **little** _petite_ triangles or six-foot-long crowd-**suited** _serving_ inventions. They may hold **accomodate** _accomodate_ peanut butter or roast beef. They may consist of **fresh** _uncooked_ vegetables and mayonnaise. Or they may be **filled** _loaded_ with **hot dogs** _frankfurters_ and saurkraut.

Did you **know** _realize_ the Sandwich Islands were **named** _dubbed_ to honor this 18th century lord? Now we call these islands Hawaii, but when Captain James Cook **arrived at** _reached_ them in 1778, he named them after his **boss** _director_, John Montagu.

Word Box
accommodate, clients, diverse, loaded, narrative, realize, stick
assembled, devised, dubbed, lured, petite, sent, uncooked
bore, director, frankfurters, meal, reached, serving

Page 85

Bring on the New!

Ann, Fran, Jan, and Nan can usually agree on the important things in their lives. Yet, when the political elections came up today, they found that they were miles apart in their thinking. Match each girl to her candidate of choice (first and last name) and decide which single issue was most important to each voter.

1. Fran, for whom either foreign affairs or finance is a burning issue, voted for neither Dobb nor Noah.
2. Ann and Jan favored male candidates, neither of whom made finance their primary issue.
3. The four voters are the one who supports Sobb, the one whose key issue is crime, Nan, and the one choosing Louis.
4. Megan's last name is either Robb or Sobb. She is a finance wizard.
5. Ann does not vote for Sobb. The one who votes for Louis is not interested in women's issues. Jan has an interest in foreign affairs.
6. Mr. Robb is strong on neither foreign affairs nor the issues of women.
7. Louis is either Nobb or Sobb.

Page 86

Crazy Cryptics

All the words in this cryptic puzzle follow the same code. A set of letters has been substituted for the correct letter in each word. All of these words have something to do with the election process. Can you figure them out?

Clues:
1. The letter H represents E.
2. The letter E represents S.
3. The letter L represents O.
4. The letter I represents P.

1. ZLYBTA — VOTING
2. ALZHOTLO — GOVERNOR
3. VHRLJOKYE — DEMOCRATS
4. JKRIKBAT — CAMPAIGN
5. HBAMYHHT — EIGHTEEN
6. JLTAOHEE — CONGRESS
7. OHIQUGBJKTE — REPUBLICANS
8. RKSLO — MAYOR
9. ULLYM — BOOTH
10. IOLRBEHE — PROMISES
11. IOLILEKGE — PROPOSALS
12. PSNRGNY — SENATOR
13. ORNGIO — BALLOT
14. YZKVE — TV ADS
15. IOHEBVHTY — PRESIDENT

"THE RIGHT TO VOTE IS, LIKE, THE CORNERSTONE OF DEMOCRACY!"

Page 87

Over There!

This day marks the end of World War I or *the Great War* as it was called then. Some people call this day *Armistice Day*. This war involved the use of trenches, mustard gas, machine guns, and tank warfare for the first time.

Match the words in the left column to the synonyms on the right. Place the appropriate letter in front of each number. Not all words in the second column will be used.

D	1. horse soldiers	a. truce
E	2. conquest	b. rations
T	3. doughboy	c. partner
O	4. armored vehicle	d. cavalry
Q	5. cooties	e. border
K	6. captive	f. victory
R	7. victim	g. offensive
M	8. camouflage	h. masses
P	9. arms	i. conflict
S	10. ruination	j. ditches
A	11. armistice	k. prisoner
G	12. attack	l. surrender
H	13. crowds	m. disguise
C	14. ally	n. uniform
E	15. frontier	o. tank
I	16. war	p. weapons
J	17. trenches	q. lice
B	18. army meal	r. casualty
		s. destruction
		t. soldier
		u. battle

ARMISTICE DAY WAS CHANGED TO VETERAN'S DAY IN 1954!

A Picture's Worth . . .

Match the words with the appropriate picture. As you write down the name of each picture in the correct spot, the words reading vertically in the bold line will spell a Thanksgiving Day message. Two of the pictures will be used twice.

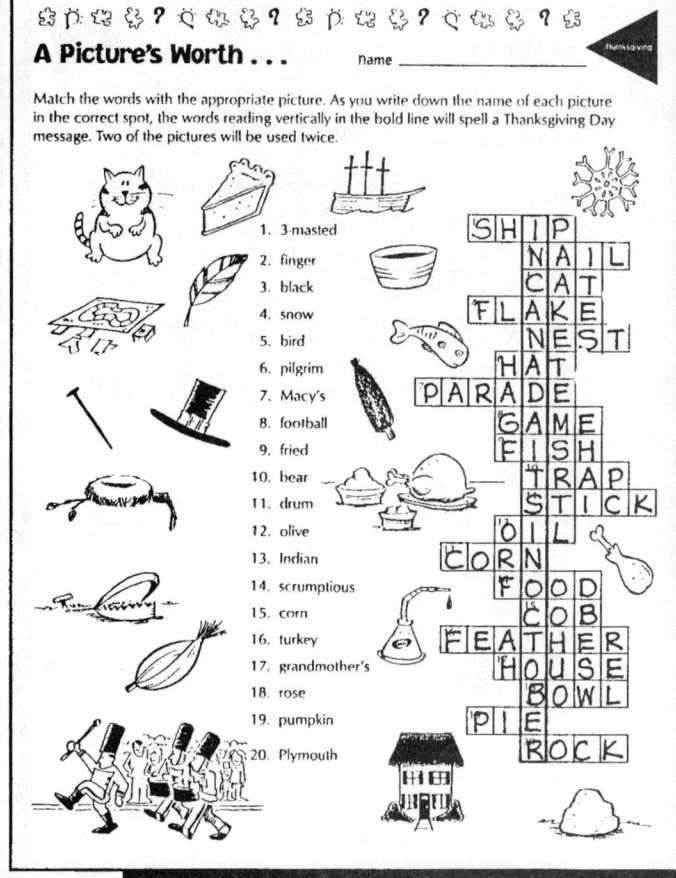

1. 3-masted — SHIP
2. finger — NAIL
3. black — CAT
4. snow — FLAKE
5. bird — NEST
6. pilgrim — HAT
7. Macy's — PARADE
8. football — GAME
9. fried — FISH
10. bear — TRAP
11. drum — STICK
12. olive — OIL
13. Indian — CORN
14. scrumptious — FOOD
15. corn — COB
16. turkey — FEATHER
17. grandmother's — HOUSE
18. rose — BOWL
19. pumpkin — PIE
20. Plymouth — ROCK

A Thanksgiving Puzzle

Find the six-letter words defined below. Then trace them in order in the puzzle beginning with the boxed square. In this puzzle the last letter of a word becomes the first letter of the next word. You will use all the letters.

Definition	Word
1. the Thanksgiving bird	TURKEY
2. color of sweet corn kernel	YELLOW
3. how a duck or goose might walk	WADDLE
4. the use of energy to do something	EFFORT
5. the serving dishes are placed on these	TABLES
6. holy	SACRED
7. trenchers, bowls, platters	DISHES
8. companionable, gregarious	SOCIAL
9. mourn or grieve for	LAMENT
10. to journey	TRAVEL
11. timber cut for building use	LUMBER
12. misgiving	REGRET
13. gratitude	THANKS
14. freedom from danger	SAFETY

THE FIRST NATIONAL THANKSGIVING DAY WAS CELEBRATED NOVEMBER 26, 1789!

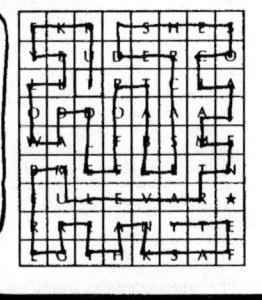

Turkey Time

Write the words which match the descriptions below. Need clues? Unscramble the words at the bottom of the page to help discover the answers.

1. FAMILY — children + parents = _____
2. EGGNOG — festive drink for the holidays
3. LOVE — emotion of great affection
4. LAUGHTER — mirth + giggles = _____
5. ORIGINAL — the first; beginning
6. WARMTH — opposite of coldness
7. STUFFING — food put into turkey's cavity before roasting
8. HAM — pig's meat
9. INVITATION — a request to come and celebrate
10. PILGRIMS — early American thankful folk

ABE LINCOLN MADE THANKSGIVING A NATIONAL HOLIDAY IN 1863!

Clues

amh	ggegon	iiiaonnttv
levo	fnuisfgt	garuhlet
iiaglnro	lafyim	hatmwr
rsigipml		

Now, use the first letter of each answer to find a word associated with this holiday.

F E L L O W S H I P

© Instructional Fair • TS Denison

IF8728 *Challenge Your Mind*

Festival of Lights

The Jewish celebration of Hanukkah reminds Jewish people around the world of an important event in their history—a miracle that happened in their struggle against a powerful enemy.

Match each word from the Word Box to its definition. The letter boxes may help you do this more easily.

Word Box

Antiochus, Hanukkah, Hallel, Kislev, Maccabees, menorah, Talmud, Apocrypha, dreidel, Judah, latkes, Mattathias, olive oil

1. the candelabrum — **menorah**
2. potato pancakes — **latkes**
3. "dedication"; also called "Feast of Lights" — **Hanukkah**
4. the Jewish literary document of law and lore — **Talmud**
5. the enemy Seleucid monarch — **Antiochus**
6. the family name of the Jewish high priest of this historical story; the name means "hammer" — **Maccabees**
7. Jewish historical and religious writings from the 1st and 2nd centuries B.C. — **Apocrypha**
8. The old Jewish priest who began this historical revolt — **Mattathias**
9. the Jewish month in which Hanukkah is celebrated — **Kislev**
10. a 4-sided top used in this celebrative time — **dreidel**
11. fuel used for the menorah — **olive oil**
12. praise psalms — **Hallel**

A Right Jolly Fellow

The legends of Saint Nicholas are old and varied. Many countries claim ownership of this Christian saint. Insert the 21 letters from the Letter Bank into the empty boxes to form words related to the saint's stories. The letter you insert may be the first, the last, or in the middle of the word. Cross out letters in the Letter Bank as you use them. The numbers along the side give the length for that line's word. Your finished list from top to bottom will give two foreign names for this saint.

Letter Bank: A A E E E E I K L L N N O O P R R R S S T

SAINT NICHOLAS IS THE PATRON SAINT OF RUSSIA, CHILDREN AND SAILORS!

Fly Away Home

Match the words and phrases in the Word Box with the correct category headings.

Word Box

aileron, DC-3, frame, jacket, propeller, sunglasses, ultralight, biplane, dip, fuselage, jet, rise, supersonic, uniform, cable, dive, glide, lift, roll, airliner, visor, B-52, elevator, glider, nose, rudder, swoop, wings, climb, engine, goggles, pedal, seaplane, controls, flaps, headphone, plunge, shuttle, cruise, flight suit, helmet, pitch, soar

Aviator Wear	Flight Actions	Plane Parts	Plane Types
flight suit	climb	cables	biplane
goggles	cruise	controls	DC-3
headphone	dip	elevator	glider
helmet	dive	engine	jet
jacket	glide	frame	seaplane
sunglasses	lift	fuselage	shuttle
uniform	pitch	nose	supersonic
visor	plunge	pedal	airliner
	rise	propeller	ultralight
	roll	rudder	
	soar	wings	
	swoop	aileron	
		flaps	

CHARLES LINDBERGH WAS THE FIRST TO FLY SOLO ACROSS THE ATLANTIC OCEAN!

IT TOOK 33-1/2 HOURS!

Northern Climes

When winter arrives in the northern latitudes, people know they must adjust to the season change. Complete this crossword puzzle about this chilly time.

Across
3. long foot gear for traversing snowy terrain
5. a precipitant mixture of rain and snow
7. the neck wrap for a cold day
9. a steamy beverage made from the cacao seed
10. frozen rinks of ice are good for this
15. a long, flat bottomed wooden sled
17. symptoms of this are coughing and sneezing
19. the supposed sleigh-pullers on December 24
20. snow wall from behind which snowball-laden warriors sally forth
21. a pile of snow shaped by wind
23. the foreclosure of academic studies (sometimes associated with 7 down)

Down
1. celestial images made while lying prone in the snow
2. chubby snow statues, like Frosty
4. melted and refrozen snow formation which hangs from roofs
5. the tubby senior elf of northern lore
6. dump _____ are used by some cities to haul away excess snow
7. a blizzard
8. this occurs when the dew point is below 0 degrees Celsius
11. large vehicles used to scrape snow from roadways
12. the solstice reached in late December
13. warm handwear utilized particularly by the young
14. a traveling condition considered a driver's nightmare
16. the seemingly lower temperature due to excessive breeze
18. long underwear
22. fuel for the fireplace

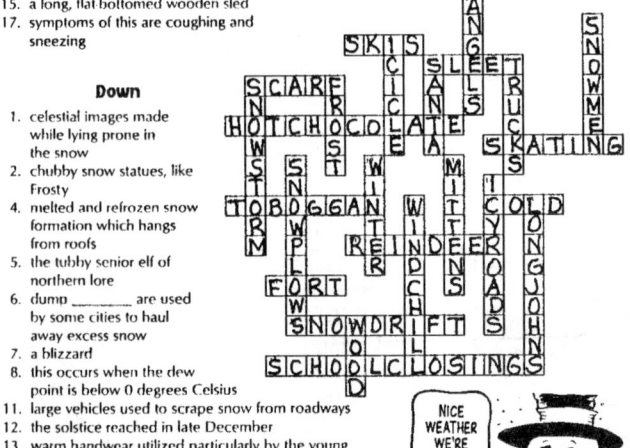

NICE WEATHER WE'RE HAVING!

© Instructional Fair • TS Denison

IF8728 Challenge Your Mind

Ho Ho... Oh No!

Find the 35 Christmas words hidden in the wordsearch below.

Do you know what Boxing Day is?

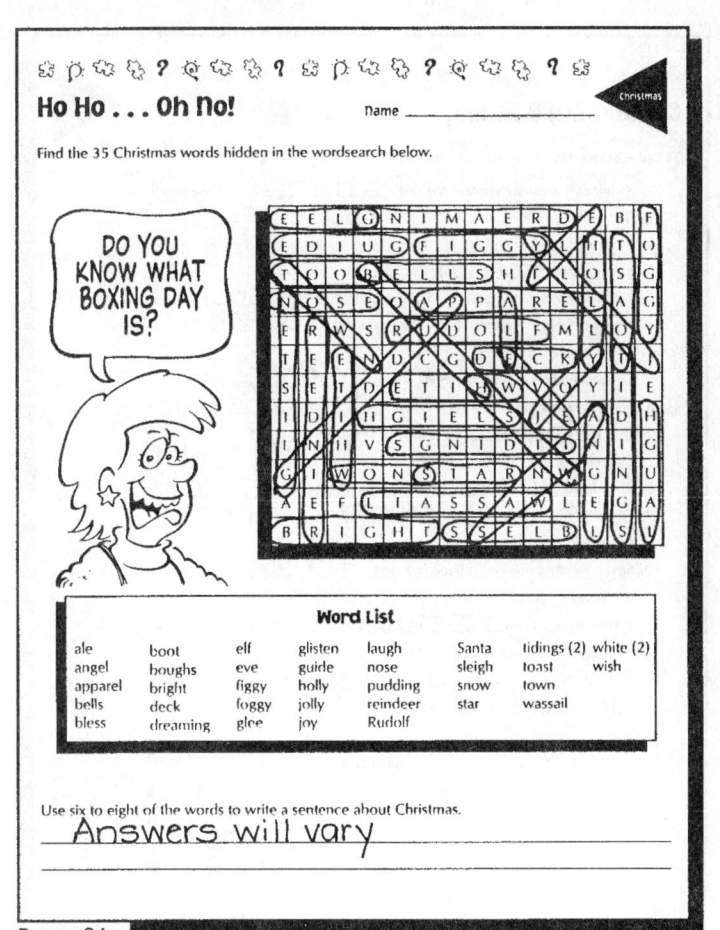

Word List
ale	boot	elf	glisten	laugh	Santa	tidings (2)	white (2)
angel	boughs	eve	guide	nose	sleigh	toast	wish
apparel	bright	figgy	holly	pudding	snow	town	
bells	deck	foggy	jolly	reindeer	star	wassail	
bless	dreaming	glee	joy	Rudolf			

Use six to eight of the words to write a sentence about Christmas.

Answers will vary

Page 96

Sing Lullaby

Match the words from the Word Box with their synonyms. Write the words in the boxes provided.

Word Box
baby, candy, carol, cold, jolly, joy, light, love, musical, peace, present, ring, rosy, sleigh, sparkle

MUSICAL — tuneful, ariose, melodic
PRESENT — gift, boon, largesse
ROSY — ruddy, flushed, glowing
SPARKLE — shimmer, glitter, scintillation
JOLLY — jocund, mirthful, festive
SLEIGH — sled, carriage, sledge
CANDY — confection, sweets, treat
BABY — infant, neonate, bambino
CAROL — chant, tune, vocalize
JOY — cheer, bliss, happiness
LOVE — devotion, fancy, adoration
LIGHT — illumination, incandescence, luminosity
RING — chime, knell, peal
COLD — nippy, boreal, arctic
PEACE — calm, repose, tranquility

Page 97

Sing We Merrily

Christmas is a time of singing. Here are song phrases both religious and secular. Choose word phrases from the list below as you complete each crossword. Be careful! You will not use all phrases on the list.

Phrase List
boughs of holly, bells on Bobtail, silent night, oh Christmas tree, good King Wenceslaus, away in manger, figgy pudding, gloria in excelsis Deo, merry little Christmas, 'tis the season, hark! the herald angels, sweetly singing, one-horse open sleigh, Rudolf the red nosed reindeer, peace and goodwill, what child is this, Christmas time in the city, sleigh ride together, your Christmases be white

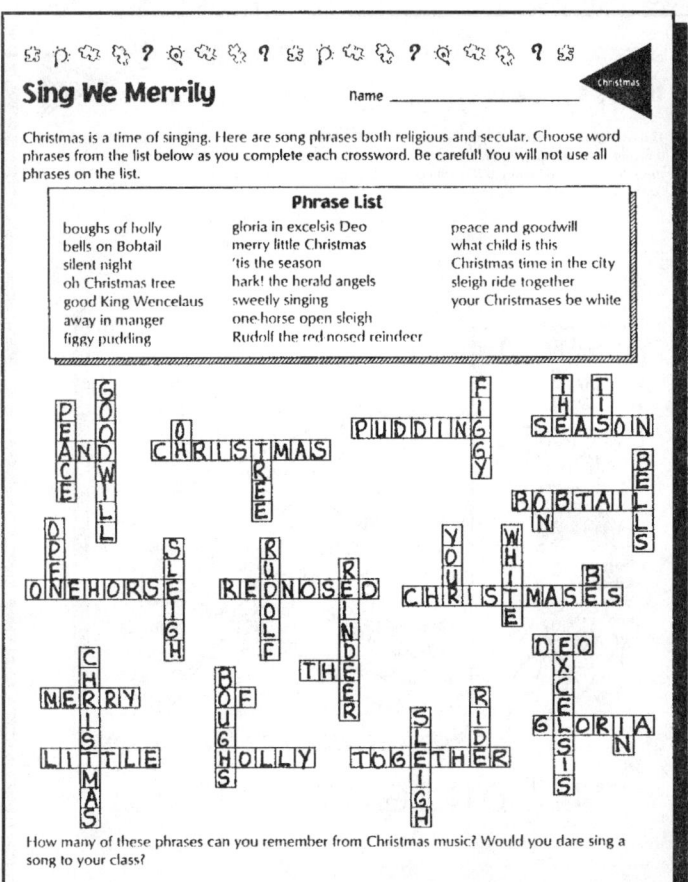

Crossword answers: PEACE, GOODWILL, CHRISTMAS TREE, FIGGY, PUDDING, TIS THE SEASON, BOBTAIL, BELLS, OPEN, SLEIGH, ONE HORSE, RUDOLF RED NOSED REINDEER, YOUR CHRISTMASES WHITE, DEO, EXCELSIS, MERRY, CHRISTMAS, LITTLE, BOUGHS, HOLLY, SLEIGH, TOGETHER, RIDE, GLORIA

How many of these phrases can you remember from Christmas music? Would you dare sing a song to your class?

Page 98

What Child Is This?

Fit the letters in each column into the boxes directly above them to form words. The letters may or may not go into the boxes in the same order in which they are given. Words may wrap to a second line. Your finished puzzle will describe one of the puzzles of the season. Ho, ho, ho!

AT CHRISTMAS EVEN
THE TIMID CHILD MI
GHT SIT ON A WHISK
ERED STRANGERS LAP

"A Christmas Carol" was first published in 1843. It's a Dickens of a story!

Page 99

127

© Instructional Fair • TS Denison

IF8728 Challenge Your Mind

Christmas Superstitions in Threes

Three words are missing from each phrase. Match the letter of the missing phrase to each sentence.

G 1. Holly placed in windows protects a ___ ___ ___.
J 2. A sprig of holly ___ ___ ___ brings happy dreams.
N 3. Bells and chimes should be sounded on Christmas Day ___ ___ ___ evil spirits.
P 4. A candle left burning all night in an empty room on Christmas Eve brings light, ___ ___ ___ all year.
O 5. Anyone who is not kissed ___ ___ ___ will not marry during the next year.
E 6. If Christmas bells toll on a Saturday, the winter will be foggy and the ___ ___ ___.
A 7. ___ ___ ___ on Christmas Day can tell the future.
D 8. A cricket chirping at Christmas ___ ___ ___.
L 9. A stranger at the door on Christmas Eve may be ___ ___ ___ in disguise.
K 10. On Christmas Eve ___ ___ ___ procession.
C 11. Farm animals compare notes on how they've ___ ___ ___ in the past year.
M 12. Ashes from ___ ___ ___ can cure many diseases.
I 13. Bread baked on Christmas Eve will ___ ___ ___.
B 14. A green Christmas means ___ ___ ___.
F 15. A girl may knock on the gate of a pigsty. If a full-grown pig ___ ___ ___ she will marry an old man.
H 16. People born the hour before midnight on Christmas Eve understand the ___ ___ ___.

A. a person born	G. home from evil	L. the Christ Child
B. a white Easter	H. language of animals	M. the Yule log
C. been treated during	I. not become moldy	N. to frighten away
D. brings good luck	J. on the bedpost	O. under the mistletoe
E. following summer cold	K. sheep walk in	P. warmth and plenty
F. grunts in reply		

Page 100

Community Building

Fill in the blanks with words from the Word Box.

1. Kwanzaa is a word meaning "the first **fruits**." It is based on the celebration of the gathering of crops in **African** countries.
2. Maulana Karenga, a **civil** rights leader and teacher, introduced this community **holiday** to African Americans.
3. During Kwanzaa one pays **honor** to one's **ancestors**.
4. The principles of Kwanzaa emphasize working **together** for the sake of the whole community.
5. This celebration focuses on family and **friends**, not religion.
6. Families may learn words in the Swahili **language**, which was developed to **improve** trade in East Africa.
7. On December 31 participants all gather for a karamu, or **feast**.
8. On a low **table** is placed a mkeka which is a **woven** mat.
9. The kinara or candle holder is **placed** in the **center** of this mkeka.
10. Seven candles, one black, three red, and **three** green, are used in the kinara.
11. Mazeo, or fruits and **vegetables**, may be set on the mkeka along with the kikombe cha umoja, or **unity** cup.
12. A storyteller may share the **history** of the family and the **legends** from Africa.

Word Box

African	feast	holiday	legends	together
ancestors	friends	honor	placed	unity
center	fruits	improve	table	vegetables
civil	history	language	three	woven

Page 101

An African Tradition Returns

Nearly 5 million African Americans celebrate this festival focus on their cultural heritage.

Fit the letters in each column into the boxes directly above them to form words. The letters may or may not go into the boxes in the same order in which they are given. Words may wrap to a second line. Your finished puzzle will point out symbols of this Kwanzaa experience.

THE FIRST FRUITS GIVE US TIME
FOR THANKS FOR KWANZAA HAS BEG
UN WE LIGHT THE CANDLES SHARE
THE CUP WITH EACH AND EVERYONE

KWANZAA WAS ORIGINATED IN 1966 BY M. RON KARENGA. IT'S BASED ON A TRADITIONAL AFRICAN HARVEST FESTIVAL!

Page 102

10...9...8...

The two lists below contain partner words. Match each word in List A with its partner in List B by drawing a straight line. As each line is drawn, it will pass through a bold-type letter. Set each of these letters in the blanks at the bottom of this page to finish this quatrain:

As you behold this festive night
With friends and kin so dear
Do give your voice with all your might
with shouts of _____

List A
1. ball
2. fireworks
3. party
4. resolution
5. friendly
6. boisterous
7. group
8. radio
9. Father
10. counting
11. Auld
12. salted
13. hearty

List B
favors
games
down
fellowship
drop
Lang Syne
Time
toast
snacks
making
nostalgia
singing
display

M I D N I G H T   C H E E R
1 2 3 4 5 6 7 8   9 10 11 12 13

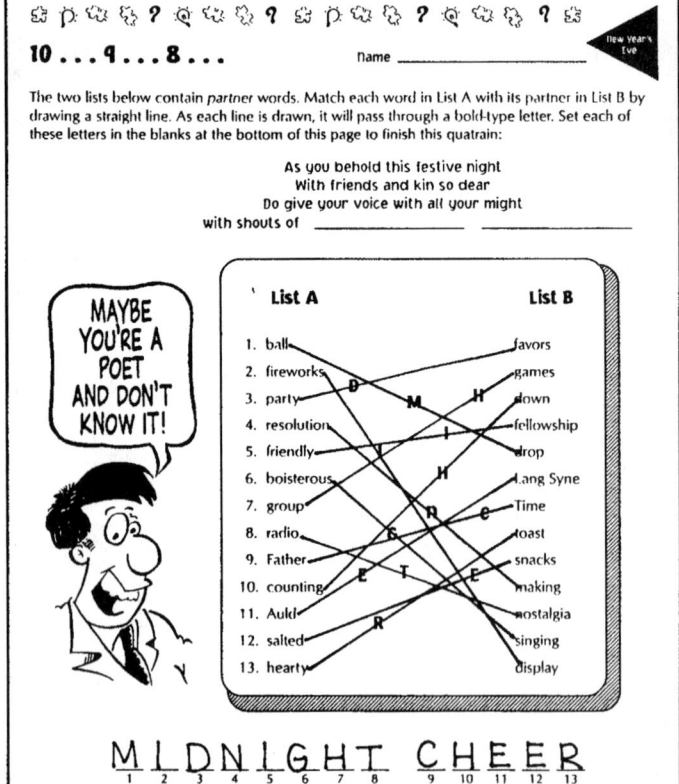

Page 103

© Instructional Fair • TS Denison

IF8728 Challenge Your Mind